La Grande Misère

Great Misery

LA GRANDE MISÈRE

Great Misery

Maisie Renault

Translated with an introduction by

Jeanne Armstrong

Zea Books
Lincoln, Nebraska 2013

ISBN 978-1-60962-034-9 paperback
ISBN 978-1-60962-035-6 e-book

Set in Constantia types.
Design and composition by Paul Royster.

Zea Books are published by the
University of Nebraska–Lincoln Libraries.

Electronic (pdf) edition available online at
http://digitalcommons.unl.edu/zeabook/
Print edition can be ordered from
http://www.lulu.com/spotlight/unllib

Introduction to *La grande misère*

by Jeanne Armstrong

Maisie Renault, 1907-2003, author of *La grande misère*, was the oldest daughter of Léon and Marie Renault, devoutly Catholic and patriotic parents who lived in Vannes, France. Maisie's older brother Gilbert was born in 1904. Léon was a professor of English before he married Marie and then worked as an insurance inspector. He and Marie had ten children together, one of whom died young. According to Guy Perrier, Gilbert Renault's biographer, Léon raised Gilbert, and probably the other children, to be fervent Catholics with a devotion to the Virgin Mary (Perrier 2001). When Léon Renault became ill and died in 1924, Marie raised the younger children with the help of the oldest, Gilbert and Maisie. The names and dates for the ten children are: Gilbert, 1904–1984; Alice, 1906–1920; Maisie, 1907–2003; Hélène, 1910–1997; Annie, 1912–1990; Philippe, 1915–1945; Jacqueline, b. 1917, a nun; Claude, 1919–2007; Madeleine, b. 1921; and Isabelle, 1923–2010.

Maisie Renault's experience with the French Résistance began when she came to Paris in 1941 to work as secretary for the network directed by her brother Gilbert, whose code name was Colonel Rémy. This group, which Gilbert named the Confrérie de Notre-Dame in recognition of his devotion to "Our Lady," was based in Paris and was one of the key intelligence networks of the Résistance. According to Rémy he was inspired to name the group Confrérie de Notre-Dame during a visit to the church, Notre-Dame-des-Victoires. He decided to place this group under the protection of Our Lady since the French kings had placed France under the protection of Our Lady (Notre Dame), then why not place this résistance group under her protection (Rémy 1948:245–6).

When Maréchal Pétain readily surrendered to Germany, many French people were shocked. On June 18, 1940, General De Gaulle made his radio speech from London urging the French people to reject the armistice and to resist the German occupation. This was followed on the actual date of the armistice, June 22, by his second more widely heard BBC speech. This speech stirred many French men and women to form Résistance groups (*réseaux*) and work toward ending the German occupation through strategies of sabotage, armed conflict and intelligence gathering.

Germaine Tillion, fellow Ravensbrück prisoner and a friend of Maisie Renault, was an anthropologist at the Musée de l'Homme in 1940. She and her museum colleagues formed a group that later was simply referred to as the réseau du Musée de l'Homme. In describing the formation of this group as well as the other groups that arose in the early period of occupation, Tillion explained that it was initially a spontaneous mass movement arising among people from a diverse variety of political orientations and social levels. She describes the Musée de l'Homme network members thus, "They were from the left, the right, the extreme left and the extreme right" but specifies that at first there were no communists because of the Stalin-Hitler Pact. Germaine explained that those joining such groups were all motivated primarily by their firm rejection of the armistice which was regarded as shameful, saying "Gaullism is the refusal of armistice," (Lacouture 2000:78-79)

The Résistance group directed by Gilbert Renault, known as Colonel Rémy, was the most important in gathering and transmitting military intelligence to the headquarters of free France in London. In *La Résistance Sacrifiée,* Alya Aglan refers to comments made by Christian Pineau, organizer for the northern zone of résistance, on Rémy as not especially interested in politics or opposing the Vichy regime but solely in his intelligence work to end the German occupation (1999:369 n.5). In his war memoirs,

General Charles De Gaulle described Colonel Rémy as shuttling back and forth from Paris to London to pass intelligence to him.

> Rémy's network, Confrérie Notre Dame, was working at full spate. For example, not a single German surface boat arrived at or left Brest, Lorient, Nantes, Rochefort, La Rochelle, or Bordeaux without London's being warned by telegram. Not a single military work was built by the enemy on the Channel or Atlantic coasts, particularly in the submarine bases, without its situation and plan being at once known to us. Rémy had, in addition, organized contacts methodically, either with other networks, with the movements in the occupied zone, or with the communists (Gaulle 1955:273-4).

Eventually Confrérie Notre Dame, like many other Résistance groups, was penetrated by collaborators, resulting in the denunciation and arrest of members. In 1942 Maisie and Isabelle were denounced and arrested by the Gestapo while staying in the apartment belonging to their brother Rémy. Their mother, their brother Philippe and three sisters including Madeleine, who was still ill from her imprisonment when Maisie returned, were arrested and released in February 1944—all except Philippe. He was deported to Neuengamme camp and died when the ship evacuating the prisoners was sunk by the British in May 1945. Their brother Claude joined the 1st Division of the Free French and fought in North Africa and Italy.

After being interned at La Santé prison, Fresnes, Romainville and Compiègne, Maisie and Isabelle were eventually deported in 1944 to Ravensbrück, a concentration camp for women that was 56 miles north of Berlin.

According to Israel Gutman, "By early February 1945, 106,000 women had passed through the Ravensbrück camp. Twenty-five percent of them were Polish, 20 percent German, 19 percent Russian and Ukrainian, 15 percent Jewish, 7 percent French, 5.5 percent Gypsy, and 8.5 percent others" (1990, 1226). Two friends, Germaine Tillion and Geneviève de Gaulle, niece of Charles de

Gaulle, were held in the *Nacht und Nebel** section of the camp, which Maisie mentions visiting in her book, *La grande misère.*

Maisie and Isabelle along with Germaine Tillion and about 300 other French women prisoners were repatriated from Ravensbrück by the Swedish Red Cross in April 1945. Maisie Renault was made an officer of the Légion d'Honneur and awarded the Croix de Guerre and the Médaille de la Résistance. In 2005, I wrote to Germaine Tillion asking about her memories of Maisie Renault. She asked her friend and Ravensbrück comrade, Anise Postal-Vinay, to write on her behalf. This is my translation from her letter, "Maisie had absolute moral principles which she applied in the terrible daily life of the camp: to never complain; to go to the limit of her strength; to help others. This absolutely correct conduct was dictated to her by an elevated sense of duty and undoubtedly by the Christian education that she had received."† (April 22, 2005)

When she wrote her account of the camp in 1947, Maisie intended it to serve as testimony of the horrible conditions and abusive treatment in this women's camp and in memory of those who did not return. In 1948, her book, *La grande misère,* was awarded the prix verité. Her book shares some characteristics with other concentration camp accounts by French women and with Holocaust survivor testimony, yet has a unique style and perspective, reflecting Maisie's middle-class, Catholic background. Moreover, it is written in the first person and present tense, organized chronologically almost like a diary, which gives it a sense of immediacy and drama that distinguish it from some other accounts of the camps, which were written years after the experience or in a more objective style.

---

* Nacht und Nebel, the Night and Fog Decree of 1941 had the intention of causing political activists to disappear, so no information could be found on their whereabouts or destiny.

† "Maisie avait des principles moraux absolus qu'elle appliquat dans la terrible vie quotidienne en camp = ne jamais se plaindre; aller jusqu'au bout de ses forces; aider les autres. Cette conduit absolument droit la etait dictée par un sens élève du devoir et sans doute par l'education chrétienne quelle avait récue."

Maisie and her French comrades in the camp created surrogate families to support one other. *La grande misère's* account of the role of surrogate families and mutual support that allowed some women to survive longer is typical of other women's testimonies from the camps.* Maisie's surrogate family was composed of French women since women in Ravensbrück would naturally associate with those speaking their language. The most frequently mentioned members of this community, Maisie, Isabelle, Denise, Suzanne and Lucienne, tried to help each other. When Denise weakens and is sent to the Infirmary, Maisie and Isabelle visit her there and Isabelle gives her a little medal. Later when Denise is transferred to another room, Maisie agrees to join her, knowing how frightened Denise is at being separated from her friends. Despite these efforts, Denise doesn't survive Ravensbrück. In the conclusion of *La grande misère,* Maisie remembers those who died in the camp.

> On leaving Ravensbrück, I did not want to look back but I was not able to forget. The physical miseries have lessened; but Suzanne so frail and especially so valiant, Denise with her bright smile, yet close to tears, Nicole with an expression a little fearful and all those that we have left, rise up suddenly in my memory marked by the acuteness of their suffering (Renault 1948:174).

Another survival strategy was to understand the camp system in order to better resist it. In her preface to Germaine Tillion's *La Traversée du Mal,* Geneviève de Gaulle-Anthonioz explains that Tillion's interpretation of the camp system immensely helped the women understand the method underlying the apparent madness. She states, "In listening to you, we were

* "This tenuous web of friendship was, in a way, almost submerged by the stark brutality of selfishness and the struggle for survival, but somehow everyone in the camp was invisibly woven into it. It bound together surrogate 'families', two, three or four women from the same town who had been arrested in the same 'affair' or perhaps a group formed within a prison cell or in a railroad car at the time of their deportation" (Tillion 1975:xxii).

no longer *Stücks*, but persons; we could fight since we could comprehend." (Tillion 2000:6). Tillion used her ethnological expertise to analyze and understand the concentration camp system in order to better resist the death and degradation which were the intended outcomes for the prisoners. In his biography of Germaine Tillion, Lacouture mentions that she cooperated with camp comrades in documenting the daily incidents as evidence which could later be used to obtain justice for victims. He refers to Geneviève de Gaulle, Denise Jacob, Maisie Renault and Marie-José Chombart de Lauwe, as those who joined with Germaine in "rebellious ethnography." (Lacouture 2000:167)

In addition to writing *La grande misère*, Maisie continued to testify about Ravensbrück by participating in the annual Concours de la Résistance et de la Déportation, an historical research competition in the French lycée system on a theme associated with the Résistance and deportation. In 1999-2000, when Maisie's health prevented her from visiting schools in her region of Morbihan, she prepared a written testimony on concentration camps for the concours on that theme.

In this document, Maisie again described the insane taken away in a *transport noir* (night transport) as she did in her 1947 book. However this time she concludes with "transport that led directly to the gas chamber" which is "now openly talked about ... swollen legs, sores, wounds signify the death sentence. Entire blocks are full of those with typhus.* They die like flies. The nude corpses, piled on carts are transported to be burned. The crematory burns day and night." (1999)

This 1999 document also provides more details on the experiments practiced on the "rabbits," specifying removal of muscles, sterilization, inoculation with typhus, burning with phosphorus. Lacouture mentions that Germaine Tillion and camp com-

* "The certified nurses instituted courses on the life of lice, their species, their habits, their reproduction, and gave an impressive dissertation on the dangers of exanthematous typhus as we were completely impotent to arrest such a scourge, we could do nothing but wait, philosophically, until we recognized the first symptoms of the typhus bite"(Dufournier 1948:31).

rades, including Anise Postel Vinay, Denise Jacob, Grete Buber-Neuman and Maisie Renault succeeded not only in taking photos of the mutilated legs of these Poles but also concealed them during selections thus enabling them to survive the camp as witnesses (2000:165).

When Olga Wormser-Migot questioned the accuracy of the prisoners' memories about the gas chambers and extermination at Ravensbrück, some Holocaust deniers used her challenge to the existence of gas chambers in certain camps to create doubt about the existence of gas chambers in any camp (Reid 2003). Because the mother of Germaine Tillion was exterminated in Ravensbrück when she was in the Infirmary, Tillion relied on the testimonies of former prisoners such as Maisie to prove the existence of a gas chamber at Ravensbrück.

There were several Ravensbrück trials from 1946 to 1948 at Hamburg, Germany. In the first trial, deputy camp leader Johann Schwarzhuber, several doctors who performed medical experiments, as well as some wardens and kapos were either executed or imprisoned. Schwarzhuber was the rare war criminal who decided, probably because his case was hopeless, to make a full disclosure and provided testimony that implicated Fritz Suhren (Strebel 2005:444). Dorothea Binz, Ober-Aufseherin mentioned in *La grande misère*, was condemned to death at the first Ravensbrück trial (Schmidt 2005). Hans Pflaum, mentioned by Maisie as the "cow merchant" and Fritz Suhren had escaped from the British but were recaptured and sentenced to death in the 1950 French military trial at Rastatt (Strebel 2005:544-45).

As described earlier, Maisie Renault met annually with students involved in the Concours National de la Résistance et de la Deportation. This program was started in 1961 by Lucien Paye, Minister of Education, with the purpose of encouraging young French students to study and create projects on the history of the Résistance and deportation in World War II. Other women mentioned in Maisie's book also continued to work for justice and remembrance of the camp's victims.

Sisters in Resistance, a documentary film made by Maia Wechsler in 2000 features a reunion of Germaine Tillion, Geneviève de Gaulle-Anthonioz, Anise Postal-Vinay and Jacqueline Pery d'Alincourt. These four survivors of Ravensbrück discuss their involvement in the Résistance, their experiences in the camp and their ongoing work for justice. In *La grande misère,* Germaine Tillion is referred to by her code name Koury, Anise Postal-Vinay is called Danielle, and Jacqueline Pery d'Alincourt is mentioned as one of the prisoners repatriated with Maisie and Isabelle by Count Bernadotte. Jacqueline Pery d'Alincourt died in 2009.

Geneviève de Gaulle-Anthonioz, an active member and later president of the ADIR (Association of Deportées and Internées of the Résistance), filed several lawsuits against Nazi war criminals. Fifty years after her release from Ravensbrück, she wrote a book about her experience, *La Traversée de la nuit* which was translated into English as the *Dawn of Hope.* Geneviève de Gaulle-Anthonioz died in 2002.

Germaine Tillion, whose mother Emily was exterminated at Ravensbrück, had been an anthropologist before the war. She published several editions of her book, *Ravensbrück: An Eyewitness Account of a Women's Concentration Camp* and was the official representative for both the Ravensbrück Amicale (Ravensbrück Association)and the Association des Deportées et Internées de la Résistance (Association of the Résistance Deported and Interned) at the Hamburg Ravensbrück trials. She also attended the Rastatt trials of camp leader Fritz Suhren and "work leader" Hans Pflaum. According to her April 24, 2008 obituary in *The London Times*, "Tillion taught at the École Pratique des Hautes Études from 1958 until her retirement in 1980. Throughout her career she remained actively committed to human rights, campaigning and performing countless missions." (http://www.timesonline.co.uk/tol/comment/obituaries/article3802321.ece)

References

Aglan, Alya. 1999. *La Résistance sacrifiée: le movement Libération-Nord.* Paris: Flammarion.

Dufournier, Denise. 1948. *Ravensbrück: The Women's Camp of Death.* London: George Allen and Unwin.

Gaulle, Charles de. 1955. *The Call to Honour, 1940-1942: The War Memoirs of Charles de Gaulle, vol. 1.* Trans. By Jonathan Griffin.New York: Simon and Schuster.

Gutman, Israel ed. 1990. "Ravensbrück." *Encyclopedia of the Holocaust* NY: Macmillan.

Lacouture, Jean. 2000. *Le témoignage est un combat: une biographie de Germaine Tillion.* Paris: Seuil.

Wechsler, Maia. 2000. *Sisters in Resistance* New York: Distributed by Women Make Movies.

Pendaries, Yveline. 1995. *Les procés de Rastatt, 1946-1954: le jugement des crimes de guerre en Zone franc¸aise d'occupation en Allemagne.* New York: Peter Lang.

Perrier, Guy. 2001. *Rémy: l'agent secret no 1 de la France libre.* Perin.

Reid, Donald. 2003. "Germaine Tillion and Resistance to the Vichy Syndrome." *History and Memory* 15(2):36–63.

Rémy. 1948. *Memoirs of a Secret Agent of Free France, vol. 1 June 1940-June 1943.* Trans. Lancelot C. Sheppard. New York: McGraw-Hill.

Renault, Maisie. 1948. *La Grande Misère.* Pontivy: Auffret et le Noheh.

Renault, Maisie. Personal Interview. 18 September 2000.

Renault, Maisie. 1999. *Temoignage de Maisie Renault.* Comité de liaison du concours de la Résistance et de la déportation. Morbihan.

Strebel, Bernhard.2005. *Ravensbrück: un complexe concentrationnaire.* Trans. by Odile Demange. Paris: Fayard.

Tillion, Germaine. 1975. *Ravensbrück.* NY: Anchor.

Tillion, Germaine. 2000. *La Traversée du mal: entretien avec Jean Lacouture.* Paris: Arléa.

LA GRANDE MISÈRE

Great Misery

Do not fear those who kill the body, and after that can do no more.

Luke 12.4

Kratz slowly crossed the deserted and sunny courtyard. As was his habit, he gently nodded his head and noisily shook his bunch of keys. Upon arriving near our group, he stared at us a moment and finally announced "No mass [this] morning, no mass".

It was the eve of August 15 and, on the occasion of major religious festivals, the commander permitted the abbot of Lilas to celebrate a mass inside the Fort of Romainville. A short while ago the *Sonderfuhrer* had recommended that we prepare everything for the ceremony tomorrow and now, according to Kratz, the mass was eliminated? At this stage of the war, such an announcement signified our departure to Germany. For three days now we have lived in agony, gathering in the courtyard, ordered to make our parcels, to unmake them, assembling again.

In their bunker, the men had set up a temperature chart. At a distance we heard the muffled booms of the canon; the Allies approached hour by hour. The *Boche** enjoyed the astonishment caused by his news. Everything about him reminds me of an orangutan, his gigantic size, his immense arms and his powerful hands, which always seem eager to crush something.

**Boches* is an aphaeresis of the word *Alboche*, from *Allemoche*, slang for *Allemand* (German) since the end of the 19th century. Used mainly during the First and Second World Wars, directed mainly at the invading German soldiers. Maisie uses this term in reference to the Nazis who occupied France during World War II.

Quite happily he clarified, "No mass ... [This] morning everyone [will go on] transport to Germany, all to die ... all to die." A cruel laugh shook his entire body as the hateful words hiss between his clenched teeth.

"Do you mock us? The Allies are at Rambouillet." Exasperated, I had spoken quickly, forgetting all prudence. His laugh stopped dead and he clenched his strangler's hands. The German hesitated but, while staring at us, his gaze undoubtedly saw well beyond Romainville and the borders of France toward the end of our voyage and he is overcome with laughter more than ever. Finally he decided to leave. As he walked, we could hear him repeat solely for his satisfaction, "All to die, all to die."

⁂

In the bunkers where we have been confined, gaiety prevailed. We waited for buses that didn't arrive. As the sound of cannons came closer and the Boches were annoyed by the delay, we sang because it was sunny. Very early in the morning, the Sonderfuhrer came bearing lists and he announced to us that, except for the sick, the medical service and some special cases, all will depart. In haste, we remade our parcels one more time and, soon after the call, we were led to the bunkers. Haunted already by the idea that they could be separated in the course of a long trip, best friends were trying hard to stay together and the old women were moving closer to the young ones. And so our group was complete. Near me were my little sister, Isabelle, Lucienne Dixon, who in the réseau we called Jeff, Toquette Jakson, Nicole, Lily, the sisters Schuppe and Gruner and Lotte who was everyone's friend. We sang so as to prevent ourselves from being demoralized by these long hours of waiting. Someone requested silence at the back of the shelter.

Through the narrow hole, one of our companions had noticed some people walking at a distance on the high mounds of Romainville. In the suddenly restored calm, she called out slowly in a strong voice "Hello over there listen to me." The walkers, who still couldn't see us, stopped. Then she continued, "All the prisoners of Romainville are leaving. Warn the Maquis. Stop the train. Do you hear? Stop the train." A woman in the group waved a white handkerchief. At that moment in the bunker, the silence weighed heavily. Then a blond and delicate Hungarian woman leaned against a bedstead and began to sing Ave Maria in a clear voice. We were all uplifted, each of us praying silently to the glorious Virgin on her feast day, confiding her grief at leaving family and her anguish in the face of the unknown. The last notes dissolved nearly into tears.

It's necessary to act quickly. We don't have the right to be sad. Nothing will prevent the certain advance of the Allies in the future. Nothing will prevent the Germans from being conquered. Our trip ahead appears to be short and we are pleased to be able to announce the good news to our dear friends who had preceded us there. The little cloud dissipated and, in the hubbub, the songs resumed. A humming of motors warned us that the time of departure was near. Kratz soon arrived, shaking his keys. But now he was somber, it was we who laughed.

The nervous Boches hurried and didn't even take any time to recount us. Quickly we were all loaded and the buses started up. At the middle of the hill, a bus stopped with a flat. The men got down to push it. Derisively one of them exclaimed, "in order to leave it will be necessary to give them a hand." Our outburst of laughter vexed the Boches, who kept quiet. They were gloomy and we full of elation. Already we were the victors. One last time we were able to look at the superb panorama of Paris. Then we're at the exit of the fort. Some civilians, gathered near the doors, watched us leave. A man threw himself toward one of the buses maybe to see a friend, maybe to call out some news; a German pushed him back with blows of his rifle butt. The man fell; the buses went past.

They crossed the city, taking some little frequented streets. Yet with our faces pressed to window-panes, we could still see some people coming and going in freedom. Finally the buses stopped. We were in the freight depot of Pantin. A long train made up of countless hermetically closed cars waits on the tracks. Without having time to realize what was happening to us, we had to descend very quickly in the midst of shouting, the noise of boots and the threat of rifle butts. Dazed, we were all thrown into a train car with a dirty floor without straw and then crammed and squeezed together. Once everyone got in, the heavy door closed and our coach became anonymous like all the others.

During six days and six nights, the train rolled along; it finally stopped in the little station of Furstenberg, which served Ravensbrück. Dirty, messy, limbs half numb, we again found ourselves in fresh air.

"All to die" Kratz had said, "All to die."

At the time of our arrival, the camp was beginning to be overpopulated and the blocks overcrowded by the evacuation of Warsaw, several different prisons of Germany and also some other camps. Transferred from block to block, looted by our Polish, Russian, German and Czech neighbors, crushed by strangers dressed in rags and worn shoes, driven away with blows of the *Blockowas'* clubs, we were mixed little by little with *Schmutzstücke** and knew the abyss of all misery.

On leaving Romainville, this August 15, 1944, we were 550 women. A little after our arrival at Ravensbrück, a contingent of our transport was sent to Torgaü. A month later around half returned to the camp and the other half was led on a commando; I lost track of these last ones. But of the 300 remaining at Ravensbrück, only 17 returned from the camp.

* literally "dirty bits," a term used to describe the wretched, hopeless persons who had abandoned all "decorum." Indeed this is the status to which the camps were intended to reduce their victims.

Arrival at Ravensbrück

August 21, 1944

It must have been barely 10 a.m. when our train stopped at Fürstenberg Station. For a long time, we walked on the sunny and dry road; then the sandy embankment gave way to some pretty chalets surrounded with verdant gardens. Suddenly the high walls of the camp appeared before us; the large gate opened, swallowed us up and only sadness remains all around us -a dark world, shacks, vicious guards.

Now evening falls and we are still there in front of the showers. We must remain standing. Nevertheless many sat on the ground. Others, still proper despite their fatigue, made a seat of their Red Cross carton. Early afternoon was spent in recovering our baggage. Our guards announced to us that our suitcases would follow in a car. Somewhat skeptical, we were reassured to see them arrive several hours later. Though we hadn't brought much, we still owned some coats, underwear and woolens. We were allowed to search at leisure in the disorder where our belongings were found. Not one suitcase was missing, which nevertheless didn't prevent them from taking all our things the next day at the showers.

Tired and resigned, we wait for the showers and the promised bed. The square becomes deserted; only police women guard us. A rumor circulates in the groups, "It is too late to go to the showers and there is no possibility of getting a bed without being clean." So this evening we will sleep right there. Disappointment after disappointment! We dreamt of this bed during our six nights in the bestial train cars. Too bad! It's best to organize ourselves as soon as possible. Immediately covers are spread on the ashy ground soiled with the greasy papers from our parcels. The suitcases are transformed into pillows and despite the blinding light of floodlights, which unceasingly penetrate the dark, we soon fall asleep.

A howling siren snatches us from this beneficial sleep. Aching all over all since the night was cold and the ground rather hard, we get up with difficulty. But we did not need to move; it was only the wake up call. It's just 3 a.m. and still completely dark. Near the kitchen groups of women wait in front of the closed doors. They return carrying heavily filled tureens. It's the coffee duty, which always starts before the wake-up sounds. Soon the square comes to life. The *Aufseherinnen* (women soldiers) pass accompanied by SS. These latter have leashed dogs. After some brief orders and whistle blows, it's the roll call. This still takes place inside of the camp. We need to wait at least two hours before hearing the siren ring again with the call to work.

The sun is now completely up. In a corner of the square, at a post that controls comings and goings, an *Aufseherin* is settled behind a little desk. Then parades like the previous day begin again, a fantastic scene that we contemplate in silence. Lined up in perfect order 5 by 5, the prisoners coming from the main road of the camp pass in front of the checkpoint. Later we learn that this call serves to inventory those who must work that day. The knitters, the sick, the night workers and the "available" workers return to the block. These latter can still be picked during the day for inside duties. As new arrivals, we ignore these rules and observe this review with astonishment. Some columns go towards the right, others to the left. Some arrive from the outside. Some others on the contrary get ready to leave. The punishment block marches past while singing some German tunes, almost chanting them, punctuated with bursts of forced laughter.

Next come some prisoners tidily attired in striped dresses and finally other columns of miserable beings in rags, often barefoot, carrying some shovels or picks on their shoulders. The sick, the emaciated, and the unsteady return to their blocks, mutually supporting each other. They are followed by the knitters and available workers. These columns appear from every direction, make a perfect turn and pass in front of the *Aufseherin* seated behind her table. The police move about, striking the stragglers with their whips. We hear slapping and someone howls. As on the previous day, the passing French shout to us, "eat everything, eat everything." This parade lasts at least an hour. Soon only the intermittent inside duties (work groups) pass on the square. The sweepers clean. Some small groups circulate carrying mattresses. Hitched to shafts, some women pull a truck overflowing with garbage while others push it—a miserable, human bunch, exhausted and soiled by all the waste that falls from time to time.

There is continual coming and going in front of the kitchens. The soup duties are already at their post; the last served will have to wait nearly two hours. Someone waves to us. It's Denise. Alive, alert, elegant despite her striped dress, she moves about between the rows of cans. We can see her radiant smile from a distance. Denise Fournaise is only 20. Last May we had to drag her away in tears from the arms of her mother, who was too sick to leave for Germany and stayed at the Infirmary of Romainville. Today the poor dear can't hide her joy at the idea of finally having some news.

Our turn arrives; we must go on to the showers. Like all those of the previous convoys, we will be subjected to an odious search and strip there. Completely nude, we wait to undergo the "hairdresser's" exam. I anxiously watch as Isabelle, now on the hot seat, leaves her test victorious. So do I. Behind us a little Breton woman cries, ashamed of the shaved skull that renders her unrecognizable. Finally the welcome shower that is our first real washing in a week! Each of us is given a very diminished towel and a miniscule piece of soap. We hear with irony that this soap must last two months. No one doubted that by then we would be very far from Ravensbrück.

Our clothes had been carefully arranged in parcels labeled with our names. In exchange, we receive discards—a shirt, trousers, and a summer dress decorated with a large different colored cross. That's all.

Thus is our status as prisoners confirmed. Dressed in our new attire, we leave and parade 5 by 5. Led by a police woman, we enter the inside of the camp, a well made little town.

However even though the quarters immediately overlooking the Lagerstrasse are clean, well-maintained, and surrounded with flowery small gardens, those inside present a more and more miserable appearance—dirty, unkempt, with window panes often replaced by old cartons. Basically the blocks in back are overpopulated. The very clean lanes accessing the Lagerstrasse are congested by a swarming crowd of tattered Gypsies, Russians with feet wrapped in filthy rags, sick women whose wounds ooze in the sun. Everyone moves along, holding at arm's length some gray ragged underwear that they are trying to dry. Some women, gathered in small groups, calmly delouse each other. Rubbish soils the little gardens planted with shrubs.

I remember a walk that I often made when I was a child. After leaving the high quarters of the city, I went to a little beach located about a kilometer away. In order to reach it we must cross a sort of hamlet built of sordid huts whose tiles were replaced by rusted sheet metal. Dirty and torn underwear dried in the gardens and sometimes the dirty and disheveled inhabitants would appear and look at us suspiciously. We had nicknamed this place the district of misery. This day of our arrival when were assigned to Block 24 and later transferred into dirtier and dirtier blocks, we have truly come to occupy the district of misery.

One side of our block had been reserved for our transport. For some time, about eight days, we were thus still among French women and this period, in comparison to the following months, was not too disagreeable. We enter the refectory, which will soon be filled with beds. Several of our friends are already there. Like them we sit on the floor. The space is so restricted in relation to our number that many must remain standing. We receive the order to await soup in complete silence. However, while whispering, we exchange our impressions. Most of us have succeeded in withholding something from the search;

a rosary, a medal, a wedding ring, jewelry, sometimes even a sweater or a scarf.

Poor Mother Guéguen is upset. They have taken her Breton costume from her and, for the first time at 65 years old, she is dressed city style in a gaudy colored cotton dress much too short for her. Thinking of her return, she already makes plans to send to Paris for another peasant outfit. She could not imagine returning to the country without her coiffe [traditional Breton headdress worn by older women]. Several months later the poor woman will die at Jugendlager.

Gentle Agnes, married only a short time, had her wedding ring taken away. She replaced it by a little wool thread.

The soup arrives, causing commotion and disputes. It must be eaten outside. Carefully carrying our mess kits, we try to leave, shoved on all sides by the others, who are eager to be served. The most fortunate grabbed some stools; many eat standing and others, very tired, resign themselves to sitting on the ashes. At this hour the sun is really hot and the coal dust, stirred by this large crowd, flies in our mess kits.

Toward the end of the afternoon, we are allowed to enter our dormitory. Recently washed, it seems clean enough but the living space is restricted. The beds, with three levels, form long rows and rise nearly to the ceiling. Three aisles, one at the middle of the room and one on each side by the windows, allow us to move around but two people cannot pass each other. A sleeping bag in blue and white square gingham covers each mattress. Five must share two beds and two covers. The small amount of space (each bed measures only 80 cm wide) and the grievances of the person lying in the middle, who is always uncovered, cause numerous disputes.

I settle in alongside Isabelle, at the third level. We have quickly realized that at this level we must be quieter. Our corner is nice; Lucienne, Lotte, Nicole, Lily, Toquette Jackson and our best friends from the convoy are near us. We organize ourselves as well as possible and chatter cheerfully. The composition of the dormitory is mixed and political prisoners, prostitutes, women arrested for vague reasons are indiscriminately next to each other. Everyone is talking, moving around, looking for a place to settle. Finally each makes a little place for herself. Conversations rise from the beds. Mme V... moans because they have taken her silver toiletries and her night-dress. She doesn't know what to wear. At least ten know the exact date of the debarkation. However no one agrees on the arranged message broadcast by the BBC. Another provokes some surprise by expressing the desire to see her husband arrested by the Allies; she clarifies that he seems to have been a collaborator. As for Lulu, she is surprised to have been treated so at the showers for her last lover was German, a very nice, handsome, and educated young man: because he spoke French and said "*merde*"...

⁂

Our block is in quarantine as it's intended to be used for new convoys. Although subject to the morning call, we are still excused from work and pass the majority of our time gossiping on our beds or waiting outside for distributions of soup. It's absolutely forbidden for us to associate with the other prisoners during this entire period. Nevertheless Denise is here already defying the police women who watch our aisles. She jumped through the window and came to snuggle up on our bed, where we do our best to hide her because her striped dress [is] likely to make her recognizable as an oldtimer.

Eagerly she listens to our news. We tell her that her mother must have been freed the same day as our departure as well as all the other sick people in the Fort of Romainville. The poor dear feels so happy that she cries with joy and immediately is seized with an immense hope. Since her equally ill father was hospitalized at Saint-Denis, he must also have been freed? We have known that he is dead for two months already but we do not have the courage to cause her such great sorrow and allow her to happily keep her illusion. During her entire captivity, she confided to us her happiness at the thought of seeing him again. Later, she learned from some camp "sources" that he is at Weimar and every month she trades her bread for a letter to write lovingly to him.

We are called outside. Those women formerly at Romainville are there on the path near the windows, Mlle Talet, Mme De Bernard, Irène, her face emaciated but still shining under her white hair, and some others. We are distraught to see them thinner, with ashy complexions and large eyes haunted by a strange expression. In their convoy, seven out of ten have been shorn. They press against the windows asking, "The news ... what is the news?" We are able to give them some splendid news. On August 15, the Allies were at Rambouillet. The battle of Caen was hard but the towns fell one after another after the capture of Avranches. The Maquis gave their utmost and liberated Brittany in several days. During our trip, we were obliged to make some extraordinary detours because the tracks were cut everywhere. At Châlons-sur-Marne, we saw a train carrying the Gestapo, accompanied by officers of the Kreigsmarine and the Luftwaffe, squeezed into the cars like animals. On August 15, it was estimated that Paris would be liberated at any moment. Even the most pessimistic predict victory by Christmas. They are delighted. Knowing us, they believe our news and their return seems very near. Their poor faces light up and they repeat, almost with devotion, "Soon France will be liberated." Thus we are rewarded for our troubles in coming to Ravensbrück.

Suspecting that we had been stripped of everything, they brought something for each of us, a sweater for one, another some stockings, a third some gloves and little by little our wardrobe became less miserable. We will greatly appreciate the kindness of these presents the next morning at roll call. It is still quite cold at 4:30 a.m. and we shiver under our little summer dresses.

⁂

This idle life lasts barely eight days. Toward the end of the month, we receive our numbers accompanied by red triangles since we are political prisoners. Black triangles are assigned to the asocials, violet to a religious sect, yellow to the Jews and green to common law prisoners (thieves or criminals). Isabelle becomes 57,907, and I am 57,908. From now on our names are nearly never pronounced. Now that we are registered, the life of the camp really begins for us, a life of work, and of camouflage. Continually on guard during this rude apprenticeship, we gradually learn how to manage.

With our numbers duly sewn on our sleeves, we notice very quickly that nothing prevents us from working. The next day right after the roll call, we rush towards the block as usual in a hurry to take our coffee and rest but the doors are closed. In a little while, an *Aufseherin*, accompanied by a *Kapo*, differentiated from the other prisoners by a red armband, appear. The *Kapo* randomly picks those in the groups that she wants to take to work. Naturally Lucienne, Isabelle and I, chatting unsuspectingly in a corner, are designated. Continuing to select, the *Kapo* arranges us 5 by 5 on the path. The required number is attained and the column moves off in the direction of the Lagerstrasse. The coffee has not yet been distributed but that does not really seem to matter. In front of the store, each receives a shovel. Still in rows, our tools on our shoulders, we go through the main gate between a row of SS who recount us. Then for the first time we leave the camp. For a distance of barely two kilometers, we walk along the splendid lake and the property of Himmler, who also owns Ravensbrück, and we arrive at a large sandy terrain. Very quickly the *Aufseherinnen* and the *Kapos* place us about two meters from one another in front of some heaps of sand and the tedious work begins.

The first woman takes some sand at the quarry and throws it to the second, who sends it back to the following and so goes the sequence. At the extremity of the line, small trucks are waiting. The last fill them and some others, after making them roll on the rails, tumble them onto a marshy terrain, which is to be filled. One truck follows another non-stop. We quickly understand that we must do the least possible while watching so as not to be spotted. When the guards approach, we take several large shovels full of sand but, when they move away, we slow down and chat while leaning from time to time on our shovels. As long as we are near French women, it goes more or less this way and the heap of sand in front of us is not abundant. Soon the guards change the teams. Then we are mixed among the Poles and the Germans, who work like maniacs. In front of us, a quantity of sand accumulates, attracting the attention of the *Aufseherin*.

Immediately she rushes up shouting, grabs a shovel and energetically shows us how to go about it. Then we are put at the small trucks and one of them derails. It is necessary to raise it with its load. The sun is already high. Aching, we lift our shovels with difficulty and try to estimate how much time passes between each load in our great desire for noon to at last arrive. Monotonous work, unceasingly exhausting, with several minutes of rest taken secretly. Finally the blessed whistle call and, shovels cleaned, our column moves off again. After passing the main gate and the SS with their census cards, we run towards our block hoping to relax a little and eager to eat as we have had an empty stomach since the previous day.

Having barely swallowed the soup, we are given orders to leave. This time we understood and we have decided not to let ourselves be picked. Some Russians have just arrived in the neighboring block. They have not yet received numbers and are therefore excused from work. Once outside, without waiting as we were advised, we immediately rush toward the roadblock of police at the extremities of our lane. Despite their efforts, they can't stop everyone. Only a few are struck by the randomly distributed whip lashings. Having overcome this obstacle, we rush into the crowd of Russians who are stationed in front of their block. Quickly we put on our scarves in the style of their country and avoid speaking so as not to betray ourselves.

Occasionally there is a stir in this milling group of people; some police are noticed. They look at sleeves to locate numbers. We thread our way from here to there, keeping ahead of the approach of danger. I remember that one of them grabbed my arm. Seeing that I was going to extricate myself, she started to pull my hair with all her strength and to pummel me with her fists. From a distance Isabelle gestures to encourage me. Giving a last shove with the energy born of desperation, I was again lost in the crowd.

Finally at the end of an hour, the knitters come down again. They go back to their blocks where they spend the afternoon making socks for the *Aufseherinnen*. This indicates that the call to work is finished. Cautiously we approach our block. We are free for the afternoon and now we only need to avoid the inside chores. Thus the days follow one another in a continual struggle in which we are more or less lucky to escape.

Sept 4. A transport of French women must take place. For several days this rumor circulates insistently and materializes when the *Blockowa*, after having conscientiously taken a numerical census, brings us to the main Infirmary for a physical. In the courtyard of the camp, we receive the order to undress ourselves and wait. Are the Germans who pass by doctors, camp functionaries? We don't know but our situation is very humiliating and we pretend not to see them. On this subject, I remember a delightful remark of Irène at Compiègne. Every morning we had a roll call but the sick and elderly women were excused from it. However, they had to stay in front of their bed so that the non-commissioned officer counted them. One morning Irène, a little tired, got up at the last minute and awaited the passing German with dignity though wearing a long nightshirt decorated with a little lace like old women wear. A prisoner exclaimed: "But Madame Tillion, you are in a nightshirt and the lance corporal is going to pass by." Irène re-

sponded with her shrewd smile, "Well, my dear friend, for me a German is just a chair!" as if to imply we could sit on him. Today we must think like her.

The courtyard is large and we are numerous. For two hours, we wait completely naked. It is very hot and our sweaty bodies are continually bumping into each other. Finally they call us in numerical order. One after another we pass into a second courtyard. There two officers, comfortably seated, stare at us from behind their monocles with an arrogant expression while joking. Two nurses examine us. One inspects our hands, the other our teeth. The medical is finished. We can dress ourselves again. For this brief exam we stayed nude an entire morning. With difficulty, we recover our clothes from the heap in a corner of the courtyard. All the clothes have been piled up together whether their owners are healthy or contagious. The next day there is another medical, which is still painful to remember.

Several days later big Elsa, boss of the work bureau, descends to our block equipped with lists. All my friends are designated to be part of the transport; from our convoy only Isabelle, Lotte and I stay with the elderly women and the sick. I later learned through Mickie, French employee at the *Arbeitseinsatz* (work bureau), that she had noticed a red circle near our two names, which signified "not to lose sight of under any pretext." Hoping to be able to warn us in case of danger, she removed Isabelle and I from the transport. Lotte stayed as well, being Viennese and considered as unfit as the old women. Mother Guéguen sees her daughter Yvette leave and is upset; but she is delighted to learn that we two stay. Among other Breton women, she feels less lost. Yet we are very sad to be separated from Lucienne, Nicole and the others. With barely time to tell us goodbye, our companions leave us and go up the Lagerstrasse.

All night they wait there for the showers, where they are stripped of all that they had acquired during their short stay at camp—stockings, woolens, spare underwear, all the treasures brought by their old friends or bought with bread.

At Ravensbrück we get our clothes thus: those who work at the stores take some clothing at their risk; some give them away; but the majority sell them with food as the currency. Stocks were made from the prisoner's baggage. As soon as they arrive, the suitcases of these latter, which often contain very pretty things, were sent to the stores. Some workers, busy with the sorting, get back as many things as possible. The on-call workers, those working at the sand to fill in the marsh, to pave the road with stones or at some other jobs of this type do not have any source of wealth. But it's different for many others. The cooks and the *Blockowa*, thanks to the food deducted from our rations, dress stylishly and still keep enough to feed themselves well. The employees of the stores dress themselves as they like and sell some outfits to eat more plentifully. Others busy at the work bureau require payment in kind from prisoners wishing a good place or to be crossed off a bad transport. Finally certain nurses sell some remedies that they obtain at the Infirmary. So it isn't unusual to see miserable, ragged emaciated creatures alongside smart women with very shiny hair, covered with silk scarves in bright colors, dressed in well-cut outfits with elegant shoes. The former, who comprise the majority, thus appear still more pathetic.

I forgot to mention one of the most important sources for this type of traffic, which concerns the boxcars or *Bekleidung* duty. Each day columns of prisoners leave to empty the boxcars in which the wealth looted from all of Europe was stored. Everything was found there; clothes, silver, ordinary dishes and precious dishes, pharmacy items, food etc. All these treasures must be classified by categories and then directed to stores all around Germany. Soon after this arrives at the unloading place, the SS and the *Aufseherinnen* begin helping themselves. The prisoners attached to this column were nearly always searched very severely at their return to camp. Nevertheless all manage to bring back something; one exchanges her coat; another who left barefoot returns well-shoed. Some even go further, taking precious objects. One of my neighbors in Block 27 ate her soup with a silver spoon with a coat of arms and secretly drank her coffee from a porcelain cup. But the food trucks excited the most covetousness. Despite the close surveillance, several manage to pass with some rice, sugar and even oil. Naturally all this booty fed a real commerce. However, a few took these things to help friends.

We have hastily gathered our parcels. This evening we must go to live at Block 23. With despair, we enter our new block, infinitely dirtier than the former. The sleeping bags have been removed and nothing insulates us from the mostly soiled straw mattresses. Moreover three persons must occupy a single bed. It's impossible to sleep flat or to turn over. Only the workers are entitled to blankets. These are distributed in the evening and collected in the morning. Many of our companions are suffering with purulent wounds and this exchange of blankets can only spread the germs and the vermin which have begun to appear.

We no longer form a very small group of French and are overwhelmed by Russians, Czechs, Poles and Germans. Among these last, the black and green triangles predominate. In the night, shadows prowl silently over the beds in search of objects to steal. To avoid being completely stripped, we put our bags and our shoes under our heads. However, all theft is not avoided because whatever falls to the lower level is immediately snatched. Dysentery begins to spread and there is continual coming and going in the dark around the "conveniences." They do not flow well and we must walk on a sticky carpet to reach them. Since our shoes serve us as pillows, a nauseating odor prevails in the dormitory. Despite these precautions, thefts multiply and bread and shoes disappear. One morning on awakening, a poor woman cries out in distress. Before she fell asleep, she had taken care to place her spoon very tightly between her crossed hands; the next day her hands are still joined but the spoon had disappeared. The only thing to do is buy another one from some thief in exchange for her piece of bread.

Lotte, Isabelle and I feel like poor lost birds. During several days we three live tightly united; then Lotte also leaves us. Her knowledge of German causes her to be assigned to an office in the camp. In the future, she will live at Block 2, one of the cleaner ones. We are delighted at her unexpected luck but she is upset at the idea of leaving the two of us in this misery.

We are not admitted to her new block but every day this faithful little friend crosses the entire camp to visit us. Very rare are the days when she arrives with empty hands. Besides, the mere sight of her smiling little face, never altered by an expression of bad temper, is a great comfort.

⁂

The small, sickly *Aufseherin* of the block, whip in her hand, passes among our rows. She strikes out while snickering. We must stay out of her way. The women recoil towards the partitions. We hear moaning. Her expression is so surly that we have derisively named her "Gracious." Now Gracious is no longer content with the terror provoked by her entrance into the refectory. She has devised something else. When we return toward the block after the roll, the doors are closed. It is barely 5 a.m. and they will open only for the noon distribution of soup, which we must again eat outside. Undoubtedly this prolonged standing is exhausting. Gracious hopes to thus defeat those more resistant to work.

This is a terrible regime for all, but especially for the old women who fall ill one after the other in these sad days of September! The mornings are very cold and woolens have not yet been distributed to us. Nearly every day we are picked for work because it's very difficult to conceal ourselves during this enforced standing in front of the block. Besides, strangers always denounce us and frustrate our maneuvers. Gracious only authorizes the distribution of coffee after the departure of the last columns so we set en route on an empty stomach. Dressed in little summer dresses with short sleeves, we shiver in the thick fog, which rises from the lake and covers the marshes. The sand is wet and cold and our freezing hands have difficulty holding the shovels. Today I again hear poor Marilène, who trembles and chatters her teeth near us. She is so frail that we make an effort always to give her the lightest shovel. Discouraged, she unceasingly murmurs "I can't I can't" with tears streaming down her face.

It's necessary not to think if we want to hang on so we talk of this and that. Each one plans her menu and shares some recipes. The time passes and finally, after several hours, a pale sun pierces the fog and returns a little life to our stiff bodies.

Any degree of hygiene seems forbidden in our block. There is no option of going to the showers or of sending some clothes for sterilizing as is done in the other barracks. Soon vermin invade us and propagate with lightening speed. Our foreign companions certainly constitute the plebeians of other countries. Those who delouse are very rare. When they devote themselves to this occupation at the dormitory or at the refectory, with disgust they throw on the ground the still living lice that they remove from their clothes.

Very few have a change of underwear. In the room, assigned for washing, at least three out of ten basins are blocked, and the clothes are piled up. Nearly all have had their wash towels stolen. Some have made one by cutting a piece from their shirt but many [women] wash with their hands. The piece of soap given at our arrival has run out a long time ago. Some have deprived themselves of bread to buy another but the great majority put up with it. While some are washing, others delouse themselves or eat there. In this room where a crowd of naked, emaciated bodies, marked with lice bites and wounds from vitamin deficiencies, jostles each other and quarrels amidst the unspeakable pile of dirty clothes, lie the dead of the block, continually splashed with dirty water while waiting transport to the morgue.

The bathroom maids interrupt our washing and demand evacuation of the room. In a hurry, clothes are collected as stragglers are chased with buckets of water. When the evacuated washroom presents a very clean appearance, the *Blockowa*, equipped with a pot of very hot water and superb soap, enters calmly and closes the door to make her ablutions in peace.

⁂

We became acquainted with Suzanne and her mother at the washroom where they were taking refuge to eat their soup. Madame Melot is already elderly and Suzanne is about 30. With their exquisite manners the two of them feel helpless in such an atmosphere. We sympathize very quickly and gradually learn of their trials. The youngest son had been killed while liberating a prison. Monsieur Melot, despite his 70 years and his exhausted condition, had been deported to a camp whose name they don't know. After a short stay at Ravensbrück, two other daughters had been sent on transport. Of the entire family, these two were the only ones to return one day to Belgium. Suzanne is magnificent, looking after her mother, who is weak and worn out. Though well-raised, she does not hesitate to use force to obtain a stool for her mother. Though timid, she dares to resist the police in order to escape from work and remain with her. Later when she is with us in the column for forestry work, each evening she brings back to her mother the little round of sausage given as supplement in order to ameliorate her usual diet.

We meet at the refectory on the rare afternoon when we are lucky in managing to not get picked for work. Seated on the edge of a bed, Isabelle, Suzanne and Denise, a born insubordinate, discuss books, travels, and music while Madame Melot escapes a little by telling me about the attractions of her beautiful property in Namur.

Near us, the *Schmutzstücke* delouse themselves and argue in several languages.

⁂

Twice this week I fainted during roll call and Isabelle, upset and standing at my side, has to leave me on the ground. Due to these instances, the *Blockowa* finally issues me a permit for a medical consultation. The two of us go to the Infirmary but the wait is very long with a sinister parade of skeletal bodies and hideous wounds. At last my turn comes to be admitted to the Infirmary. It's necessary to have at least a temperature of 39 degrees (102.2°F). Perhaps my extra fatigue is irrelevant but my temperature is 41.3 degrees (106.3°F). Given a terse order to "Wait outside," I remain there for 5 hours barely standing. Isabelle, in tears, has been forced to leave me and return to the block. I lay down exhausted at the Infirmary 10 where they have taken me. I have acute dysentery but no one bothers with me. A sick neighbor informs me that this is customary and gives me some aspirin. The next day I receive a tablet of Tannin.

The lanes bordering the blocks of the Infirmary are difficult to access, especially at noon. Despite that, Isabelle comes to visit me at the window every day. The two of us live in fear of a transport that would separate us. I am worried to hear some shouts in the night. My friends reassure me that these are the insane. I notice them the next morning. It is frightening to see them kept in a room. They seem like lost souls with shaved heads and with emaciated limbs sticking out from a simple twill shirt. Even less nourished than us, they are dying of hunger and continually fight among themselves. They stare into space. From time to time, a truck comes and takes them in a "transport noir" (night transport).

During the night of November 10-11, 1944, a sudden noise makes the sick of the Infirmary tremble. My friend Madeleine Laurent is abruptly awakened and looks out the windows whose shutters hadn't been closed. At this moment, the moon pierces the heavy clouds and she sees a truck waiting in the lane. Abruptly the door of Block 10 opens. The insane, shivering under their thin shirts, terrorized by the ferocious barking of some dogs at their heels, and pursued by the SS, whose massive silhouettes were enveloped in woolen coats, rush into the vehicle. The *Aufseherinnen*, heads covered with black hoods, truly looking like evil angels, help the phantoms to ascend. Dominating the commotion, the sharp voice of an old woman, a victim of vengeance, cries desperately, "I'm not crazy, I'm not crazy." Nevertheless, she was loaded like the others, and the truck left for its sinister destination. In the suddenly restored calm, a complicit darkness again oppresses the camp. These unfortunates were very soon replaced.

After several days, I still have dysentery but my fever has lowered. They discharged me from the Infirmary and I returned to Isabelle's side. We are overjoyed to be together again. We hide more than ever because I'm still too fatigued to work. As danger approaches, we jump out the windows to run toward another block, alright for awhile but facing the same peril an hour later. We pass experts at punching and kicking.

⁂

With arms extended, the *Blockowa* bars the entrance of the dorm, preventing the waiting horde from entering. Early in the afternoon, we were warned that it will be necessary to squeeze together in our beds because some prisoners were waiting. We were already three on each mattress and 300 women were expected. Now they are here and impatient to enter. They come from the punishment block of Auschwitz. Nearly all are Germans, with the majority wearing a green triangle. For a long time, the *Blockowa* keeps them in check with great difficulty. Suddenly her arms come down. Immediately there's an indescribable rush. The new arrivals, shorn, eyes haggard, hurry into the dormitory. In the blink of an eye, the beds are invaded. They jump on us, using hands and feet and pulling our hair to dislodge us. We defend ourselves with our remaining energy. Suddenly the light goes out. The battle continues in the dark. Someone cries out, "Help me." A French woman is nearly strangled. Near us a new arrival coldly explains. "At Auschwitz we never knew whether we would be alive the next day. We want to sleep this evening; if it's necessary, we will kill someone but we will sleep." Finally everyone finds a place somehow or other, often four per bed. Miraculously, we keep ours. Later, I learn that Mother Guéguen, too old to fight, had to sleep on the ground as did many others.

Nearly each evening we go back to Block 15 after the return of the work columns. So as not to be noticed by the *Blockowa,* who would chase us, we furtively slip into the dormitory. In a short visit with Mme de Bernard, Irène and Mlle Talet, they give us news from the German newspaper, that is read in their block. We comment on it with them and try to read the truth between the lines. They are full of hope and we return to our block comforted. Conscious of our destitution, we refuse to sit on their beds, as they invite us to do, because we fear giving them our vermin.

Achtung! The command explodes abruptly. It's the *Aufseherin.* But today she has devised another game. She does a search. It's necessary to empty our bags in front of her. Pitilessly, she seizes objects acquired with a thousand difficulties. Numbly we throw on the tables those things to which we are most attached. Finally she decides to leave. We happily collect our few spared things. After 10 minutes pass, *Achtung,* she returns. The search recommences. Calmed by her departure, we have put back in our bags what we had been able to save the previous moment, but the spared objects disappear. She pockets those that seem to her to have some value. For more than an hour, the game continues. She retreats, comes back and recommences. We feel exhausted, depressed. *Achtung!* Here she comes again, laughing.

An SS passes on a bicycle in the lane. With a glance of the

eye, he sees the scene, the hunted expression of the women. He can't resist. *Achtung!* His guttural voice makes us cringe. Releasing his bicycle, he jumps on the table near the window. Enormous, he looks cruelly at us. Those who didn't see him arrive are nervously startled. Encouraged by his presence, "Gracious" searches with still more relentlessness. She discovers a small medal that I had managed to keep, throws it to the ground, and steps on it. In a little while, she steals the compact that mama gave me for my saint's day. It was very difficult for me to give up this precious memento. Finally she decides to leave in the company of the SS, both of them laughing.

After their departure, we collect our belongings. The inventory is quickly done. Nearly nothing is left us. Thread, needles, soap, a change of underwear all disappeared. Desolate, we contemplate our little bags made from a shirt end, which appear even more pathetic since they are now so flat! In her corner Mother Guéguen, relaxed, laughs all alone. With hands crossed on her stomach, she stared at the *Aufseherin* with her cunning peasant gaze all the time during the search. Though several little things had been stolen from her, she at least succeeded in keeping in her belt 30,000 francs and two gold watches. She had shielded these items with consummate skill from all the searches that the guards had made her undergo at the different prisons where she has been. In fact, I really tried to convince her how dangerous and useless it was to keep such things at Ravensbrück but, a true countrywoman, she insisted on keeping her savings. Now she is delighted to have won once again.

We are all exhausted and our old women are finished. Mme Elbard dies first, during the roll call. The next day we transport Mme Boulloch to the Infirmary on a stretcher. Three days later she has stopped suffering. Next it's Mlle Vachon. Despite her extreme weakness, she was forced to go to roll call. But it's necessary to nearly carry her there and to support her when she sits on the stool that the *Blockowa* permitted her to take along. Today she feels very bad. All day they let her lie on the ground in a corner of the refectory while they strive to obtain her admission to the Infirmary. Later that evening we hear the response of the Infirmary: "Women of a certain age are no longer admitted. They must remain to die in the block." We transport her to the dormitory. As the poor woman relieves herself, the *Blockowa* removes her mattress, which might be dirtied, and we must lay her right on the planks. She already has the rigidity of a corpse. Only her eyes are still alive. The unfortunate woman gives off a dreadful odor. She lies on the ground floor and we are bothered by it at the third level. Her neighbors remain on the same row, eating and sleeping there.

We can't leave her to die so alone. I lean over her. "Mademoiselle, think of God. He is near you. He will not abandon you and we will pray for you." — "Thank you ... have you any news?" The voice is strange, distant. She speaks only with great difficulty. Her emaciated hand grips my arm and her eyes fix me intently. "It is very good, we will return soon." The poor clenched mouth tries to smile, then she pleads, "Some water." I prepare to go find some for her but her neighbors freely express their indignation. "Some water! With her dysentery. Do you want to kill her?" I am weak enough to obey them. The next morning the *Blockowa* excuses the sick woman from roll call. We go to tell her this but she has died in the night. It is too late to lower the eyelids on the large staring eyes. Her transport to the morgue finally takes place in the evening.

Denise has lost her smile and her vivacity. Yet a short time ago, she leapt like a young deer across the police cordon. Her complexion leaden, eyes shadowed, she only drags herself around painfully. Upset with her condition, we advise her to go for a consultation at the Infirmary. Since her fever is very high, they agree to hospitalize her.

⁂

Toward mid-October some coats are distributed in all the blocks. With pleasure we try those that have been provided for us. Isabelle's almost fits but Suzanne slips hers on with difficulty, much too tight. already she can foresee that it will be impossible for her to wear a pullover underneath. As for mine, it is so loose-fitting that I can wrap it around me like a blanket; moreover it strikes my heels. While turning around, I see Josiane burst out laughing at my grotesque appearance; she kindly offers to shorten it to make it more elegant. I am wary to accept because, as it is, it partly covers my naked legs and soon it will be very cold. I use it the first time at garbage duty under a driving rain. Isabelle, who didn't see me leave, is anxious all morning about my disappearance.

Picking up the garbage of the Infirmary, I see a woman carried on a stretcher whose head is wrapped around with bloody cloths. With an instinctive gesture, she still tries to protect her face, which is all swollen, her wide-open mouth exposing blood-stained jaws. But the bearers are unfamiliar and I was never able to know what drama had happened.

Despite all these depravities we still kept some illusions. Thus it is that the day when Isabelle and I were designated for kitchen duty, we felt an unadulterated joy. The kitchen, earthly paradise of Ravensbrück, was inaccessible to the French. All the while following the policewoman, we mutually congratulate each other for this unexpected luck and are full of projects. Better nourished it would be possible to resist and maybe we could help the others a little? We become disillusioned soon enough. Our work takes place at the door of the temple and consists of filling some enormous crates with red cabbages and lowering them into a cave. Taking handfuls of freezing cabbages, while filling heavy baskets which we lower, raise and lower again during several hours. What a cushy job! After a short time, we are exhausted. However to fortify ourselves with vitamins, we graze on several cabbage leaves each time that we are in the cave.

Only Polish women, who have Herculean strength, work with us. A truck filled with 5 tons of potatoes arrives. Two Polish women climb onto it while some others get ready to lower the hooks that hold one of the vehicle's flaps. We two are designated to support this shutter so that the potatoes do not discharge too suddenly. A brief order in Polish, the hooks lower. With all our strength we try to prevent this mass from falling on us, but the weight overwhelms us. Isabelle collapses under the surging potatoes while I brace myself to subdue the violence of their fall. Fortunately some Polish women come to our aid and prevent a catastrophe. They look at us with the most profound scorn. As it is already late, they discharge us from the duty. Isabelle escapes with some aches and I have torn the skin of my arm. Thus ends a beautiful dream.

Night has completely fallen. Furtively we slip into the lane of the Infirmary where Denise is being treated. Since she left us, we have not been able to have news of her. Luck is on our side; the police guard is not there. Already we can see groups of prisoners who speak to the sick. We hasten our step and call softly at all the windows. "Denise... Denise." Finally here she is. With a great effort, she gets down from her bed and approaches us. Her thin little face lights up with a beautiful smile. She doesn't know what she has but every evening her fever rises and surpasses 40 degrees (104°F) but they do not give her any remedy. Maybe it will go away by itself? We try to comfort her by telling her the rumors of the camp and also the definite news from Lotte, which continues to be good.

The poor child regains hope but suddenly her face contracts horribly, her eyes become haggard! She moans, "I feel sick ... I feel sick." Her hands cling to our arms, she clicks her teeth and her legs weaken ... her eyes roll in her convulsed face. My God! She is not going to die there in front of us when we can do nothing for her! In the distance some shouts ring out. The police woman is returning. The visitors disperse like a flight of sparrows. It's necessary to escape. I murmur: "Denise my dear go put yourself back in bed." But she can only implore: "Don't leave me.... Don't leave me." A nurse goes among the beds. I call to her, "Please madame this poor woman is not well. Put her to bed." They take her in just enough time. She collapses. However the pathetic voice still moans, "Don't leave me.... Don't leave me."

Now it's necessary to go quickly. If we are caught, it's the punishment block. Thanks to the dark, we slip into the Lagerstrasse, saved yet another time. Upset, we walk in silence. No longer able to keep them to myself, I reveal my thoughts. We can't abandon Denise. Tomorrow we will come back. We will jump through the window and go to her bed if she's still alive. Isabelle replies simply, "I did not dare to ask it of you."

The next day at the same hour we again slip into the forbidden lane. Here is her window. Will she still be there? "Denise" A little silhouette raises up with difficulty on a bed. It's her. She still lives! "Don't move." Quickly we step over the window. Two sick people allow us to slip by their beds up to the center aisle. We are finally near her. She has been prohibited from moving, but she feels better. Yesterday evening the nurse gave her an injection because her heart was failing. Isabelle gives her a little medal that she has carefully guarded. Delighted, the poor dear looks at it and holds it tight in her thin hand. "Thank you, oh Thank you." But it's necessary to leave her. We promise to return tomorrow. She smiles again, appeased. But the next day no one responds to our call. Her fever still high, Denise was transferred to the main Infirmary to stay there under observation and we no longer have any news of her for a long time.

Our block is overpopulated. The supplies become insufficient. It is now impossible for us to have individual mess kits. "Gracious" has thus decided that these will be passed from one to another without it being necessary to wash them. Some among us have tuberculosis and syphilis. Unusual noises at night reveal that some are lazy in going to the toilets but we are hungry.

⁂

The authorities are disturbed by the invasion of vermin, which has descended on our block. The delousing service enters into action. The old women fear for their hair. They can't accept being shorn. As best we can, we help them to examine their clothes because they no longer see clearly enough. Unfortunately this work takes very long and we don't have much time available. Lotte lends me a fine comb, while giving me some recommendations because it belongs to one of her friends. At Ravensbrück, it is a most precious object for everyone. In turn, we inspect our hair but the damage is already too great and we are overflowing with lice. One evening on returning from work, we find Mother Guéguen in tears. She has been shorn. She moans, "At my age it will never grow back. How can I now hold up my coiffe." The lice succeed in demoralizing our poor old women.

Then the war drags on. October is already well advanced and nothing is decided. They had so much hope leaving Paris in August. Now they doubt that they will ever see France again. And won't all they had left there have vanished? All our efforts are aimed at lifting their morale. The young women often are magnificent. Near me Mme Lachaud, a farmer from Landes, laments. She confides in me while crying. "Do you think that the Germans have burned our farm? They will have taken all our animals. Such a fine herd, 80 head. They will have taken everything from us. What will happen when we return? Nothing will be left for us." But her daughter who is only 17 sits up proudly, "All the same, mama, the land will remain for us."

At the time of our arrival, Sunday afternoons were spent in inactivity. For awhile, the Germans have had the habit of occupying these hours of relaxation with a general call. This general call was horrible for all. Much longer than the regular call it sometimes lasted the entire afternoon. I remember in particular having stayed there one time from 3 to 11 p.m. Except for the sick in the Infirmary, everyone must attend it—children, the sick in the blocks. Stools were not allowed there. During one of these calls, an *Aufseherin* felt pity and permitted two of us to return a dying person to the block. But from a distance, the *Ober-Aufseherin*, saw the scene. Vociferiously she ordered the sick woman to be replaced in the rows. She died there before the end of the call.

⁂

Isabelle and I pensively watch six children who head for the Lagerstrasse. The oldest has made them place themselves in a row and now, representing an SS, he marches at the head of the line. One quite small child can't follow very fast. The boy retraces his steps and threatens with his stick. There are many children in the camp—all of Gypsy or Jewish origin. In the morning after the roll call, we can see them descend from the kitchens equipped with a small can of milk. They benefited also with a special soup, a little thicker. They lived in the same block as their mothers. But one day all of them were taken in a transport. The area of the block rang out with children's cries. Some were at least 14. Others were quite young. The boys and girls lived in common with the women. Very quickly they learned to be resourceful and to steal. On returning from Rechlin, we learned that many of these unfortunate little ones had been gassed. Some sterilization experiments had also been practiced on those from 9–14 years old.

Dysentery has become more and more devastating. Again they accept the old women at the Infirmary. Since they never leave there, it's evident that it hastens their death. Among them all, Mme de Laprade seemed the best able to endure, even though very old. I had noticed her at Romainville for her still rosy complexion that she owes to her English origins. Meeting her one day in the streets of Ravensbrück, I complemented her on her courage. She confided to me then with great simplicity—I have a great son who waits for me in France. I want to return. But a short time later, the illness reaches her. I go to see her in her block. Under the blanket, I can discern a little silhouette all curled up. She softly apologizes. "You must tell my son I have been struggling to last ... but it was too hard for me. I'm exhausted." Several days later she passed away without suffering. On my return to Paris, I would learn that her son also died from deportation.

Mme Raspilaire, the most senior of the camp, dies a little later. She was also thinking of her son. As he loved grand promenades, she compelled herself to make the tour of the courtyard a certain number of times to stay in shape so she would still be able to accompany him. Toward the end, exhausted, she cheated quite a bit and the last tour was nearly diagonal ... but with all her strength she wanted to last. Ravensbrück conquered her in turn.

Mme Monnet, Mme Audibert, Mme Labussière, all the old grandmothers died after several days of illness. Without being doctors, we could recognize those who have no more than a few days to live just by seeing their slightly fixed stare.

Irène is worried by the increasing number of deaths and tells me one day, "It's for you young ones that these roll calls are depressing. At my age I get used to it more easily."

The fire of the crematory oven often rises to several meters and a burnt odor spreads through the camp.

⁂

Several days ago Lucienne and the others came back. They felt much better at Torgaü than at Ravensbrück and in fact their appearance is not as bad as ours. They have only one desire, to go somewhere again. Their desire is soon realized. A new transport gets ready. While they wait, we try hard to find them some woolens. I give Nicole a scarf. I had inspected it well but she returns it to me with disgust: she has just seen a louse on it. Poor Nicole always so well-groomed. At Torgaü, the blocks were clean and she has not yet become familiar with vermin. When I see her again several months later on her return from Petit-Koënigsberg, dozens of lice run over her clothes but she is then so exhausted that she no longer pays any attention to them.

The announced transport takes shape. The *Blockowa* gathers the prisoners in front of the blocks. Isabelle and I, still suspicious, stay nearby and watch the authorities from a distance. Here is the "cattle merchant." We have thus nicknamed a German officer, who is named Pflaum and who designates the able women for transports. He gauges them, evaluates them exactly as if he were at an animal fair. Generally when the destination of the convoy is a factory, the director of the firm accompanies him and the two of them make their choices in the slave market. The salary of employed women is paid to the camp of Ravensbrück by the factory owner and then becomes one of Himmler's sources of revenue. Today only an *Aufseherin* and big Elsa accompany Pflaum. So those departing are not destined for this type of work.

For several minutes, the two of us are very tempted to take a place in the ranks so we can accompany our friends but, in this case, we would have to abandon Denise. What would she say if she didn't find us on leaving the Infirmary? Moreover her mama has entrusted her to us. So we decide to stay where we are. As we have foreseen, all our friends are designated. The majority of French from our block leave as well. All are delighted because it's going to be a very good transport according to the rumors that circulate in the camp,. They will be better fed, cleaner and the work won't be too exhausting. The truth is quite different but we will learn this only at their return. Petit-Koënigsberg was a disaster. Hard work on a chalky plateau exposed to freezing wind wears them out. When they come back to Ravensbrück in January many are missing at the roll call and the survivors were so exhausted that nearly all of them die soon after returning to camp.

Lucienne stays with us. At the medical check-up, they discovered that she was coming down with scarlet fever and she was immediately hospitalized at the main Infirmary.

⁂

Since our arrival at Ravensbrück, we had been part of the available workers. At the end of October, we enrolled by chance in a permanent column. That morning as usual, we two sought to conceal ourselves while hiding this time among the sick. But big Elsa saw us and, with authority, pushed us towards a column that we had noticed earlier. The *Kapo*, tall, slim, dark, didn't belong to the group controlling the work at the sand, and when we go through the large gate without receiving tools as usual, we were very puzzled as to where they were taking us. A quick and jaunty walk along the road bordered with pines, the sun rising behind the trees, the joy of having one's arms empty, all contributed to giving us a sense of happiness.

After having covered several kilometers, they distributed shovels and picks to us and we had only a very short walk before arriving at the work places. On all sides, the forest surrounds us. To see only trees, to walk on a carpet of moss, to smell this slightly moist odor that rose from the undergrowth was nearly freedom for us. Quickly Hilda, our new *Kapo*, explained the work to us. It was a mater of extracting the stumps from the vacant ground on which we have stopped. Hilda had her friend Maria who spoke a little French, tell us how happy she was to have us in her column because she loved France very much. Maria explained the following to us: that Hilda had been arrested for having been the mistress of a French man.

Undoubtedly this was the reason that she had so much sympathy for us.

The work, performed continuously without a break, was certainly very hard but Hilda had advised us not to hurry while telling us to be careful not to be noticed by the *Aufseherin*. So that we are more quickly initiated, she placed Isabelle and me near a half extracted stump. As this end of autumn was beautiful and the sun still warm (the early morning cold occurs on the walk), we found nothing better than to sit at the base of the open hole dug for this extraction. The soup was served on the site. It was thicker and more abundant than that of the block. Moreover, we received some potatoes. On returning in the evening, they distributed a supplement to us -two slices of bread, a round of sausage and a flimsy portion of margarine. Our companions each bring a little firewood and we learn that they also obtain some supplementary soup from some *Blockowas*, desirous of having a means to cook their little dishes,

We were enrolled in the *Holzkolonne* or wood column and we were considered to be strong workers. The wood cut by us was used in the kitchens' fires so we did not work for the war. Life seemed easier.

⁂

Suzanne is now one of us. Being relentlessly pursued in her block, she had to resign herself to work. Some other French women have joined us: Andrée, Françoise "Big Jeanne" and Anna "the Breton." Anna is so gentle and so economical that she always keeps a little bread set aside as she is very afraid of being without some and yet so kind that she is always ready to give a slice to the most hungry. We are divided into two teams and always work together with the same ones. Hilda permits us a royal peace. Sometimes she brings us a little bowl full of potatoes.

The stumps to be extracted are very large and their roots sink deeply in the ground. We saw and chop the arms that prevent us from digging our hole. This sometimes reaches 2 m 50 cm before we can topple the pivot, which still holds the tree in the ground. When the enormous stump is finally freed, two companions come to help us and the five of us make it lift up and topple outside the hole. It is the most delicate point of the work because we don't possess ropes and have only our arms to lift this mass. Despite our inexperience, not one of us was ever injured. Our former site was abandoned and, since a short while ago, we work at an area located more at the heart of the forest. While digging, our glance falls on the tall and somber pines that surround us. When the sun is strong enough to prevent us from being too cold, we talk hidden at the bottom of our hole. Andrée speaks of music; Françoise shares some recipes. She knows some delicious ones! When my head surfaces, Isabelle affectionately waves to me from a distance.

During this time, the *Aufseherin* flirts with the SS guard and we have the good fortune to have one who adores women. When by chance the two of them prepare to make a round, Hilda approaches and warns us. They hear no more than the squeek of saws. On returning to the block in the evening, we have a snack with bread and sausage and Suzanne struggles to come near the stove, so as to toast the bread slices for her mother. Mme Melot listens to our account of the day and happily eats the warm bread filled with paté. Near some trees we had discovered a little corner strewn with blueberries, leaves turned red by autumn. We made three bouquets from them for our friends of Block 15. Irène, Mlle Talet and Mme de Bernard are all three knitters and never leave the camp. Their weary eyes see only the ashes that cover the ground. They contemplate our little bouquets with delight.

But happy days always have an end. Hilda is dismissed from her duties by the denunciation of a little German named Elsa, her right arm and her friend. Elsa becomes our *Kapo* and then all changes. Before leaving, Hilda had distributed some new clothes to us: overalls, a striped dress and some sturdy shoes with wood soles. These are soon very useful to us. The season advances and very often we work entire days under a driving rain. The weather is so bad that they permit us, while eating the noon soup, to enter into a sort of haystack, which is hollow inside. Humidity oozes from the walls. We eat standing in the dark. Our clothes stick to our bodies and soon we are shivering. Three little Russians seated at the entrance of the haystack sing some melodies of their native land. The rhythm transforms them. They laugh and clap their hands. It seems to us to feel a little less cold.

The surveillance on the site is tightened. The big SS no longer comes. *Aufseherinnen*, accompanied by dogs, replace him. No longer busy whispering sweet nothings, they harass us continually.

⁂

Night falls, a thick and cold mist rises from the ground and envelops the copse. The work-day is ended and we follow the return path with difficulty. The *Aufseherin* walks behind us, accompanied by her dog Azow, a big brute with a ferocious appearance. We know that he could kill us on an order from his mistress. The railroad line that we must follow to reach the road of the camp soon appears. The path becomes narrower, the rows scatter. I find myself among the last. The German is bored and seeks to distract herself. She amuses herself by arousing her dog against us. Azow, irritated by her shouts, approaches me and bites my leg exactly at the place where the rag, that serves me as a stocking, is torn. He does not do me any harm but the contact of his teeth on my skin unnerves me. Nevertheless without saying anything, I continue to walk. The *Aufseherin* shouts louder, stimulates him. I feel this mass behind me. A simple push and he would knock me over. A little anxiety gnaws at me but I don't want to scream.

The game continues over several dozen meters. Tired of my feigned indifference, the *Aufseherin* turns her dog against an unfortunate woman, who is startled and starts to howl with terror. Delighted with her victory, she bursts into uncontrolled laughter. Never let her see that we are afraid no matter what the danger.

⁂

On November 10, snow starts to fall. When we leave the camp, a thick carpet already covers the ground. It adheres to our thick wood soles and walking becomes difficult. We constantly stop to tap our shoes against each other to get rid of this load which makes us stumble. Our guards are annoyed and strike the latecomers. At the middle of the site, the *Aufseherin* has lit a big fire. She has a good time with Elsa, toasting some pieces of coarsely buttered bread. The glow of the fire is reflected on their boots and lights their hooded forms, draped in comfortable mantles. The superb surrounding forest, enshrouded in snow, oppresses us. We gaze desperately at the pale sun passing behind the trees. As it moves from fir to fir, we count the hours.

⁂

Elsa knows that it is impossible for us now to find dead wood. Since she figures out that we use one of the stumps to make bundles of sticks, she orders us to report only every other day, thus depriving us of our supplemental soup several times a week. Since several days ago, we are charged with returning the empty tureens, which contained our soup. These are extremely heavy large thermal pots. Stumbling in the snow, bent double by this weight, we force ourselves not to fall.

Some empty cars returning to camp pass us.

⁂

We are assigned to another block. After returning from work, we have just learned this from the policewoman posted on the square. Immediately Suzanne is in a panic, "Where is her mother?" Are they going to be separated? It's impossible to know anything at the moment. We receive an order to wait in straight rows in front of the commander's office until we are given the number of our new block. Near us, Suzanne cries silently. A fine rain starts to fall. It's now completely dark. Our soaking wet clothes weigh heavily on our shoulders. The square is almost flooded. The water isn't able to drain into this marshy terrain. Near the kitchens someone moans on an abandoned cart. In the beam of the floodlights, we can see two skeletal legs swaying. The moans increase, and we hear a splashing sound. Because of swaying, the shadow fell in a puddle of water where she continues to moan. Two police go towards her, look with curiosity, then leave again.

Finally the moans stop. Undoubtedly the unfortunate woman has ceased to suffer.

We haven't been allowed to move. It's very late. We are tired. We are cold and hungry. Finally we are given our posting. We are assigned to Block 29, side A. While Suzanne leaves to search for her mother, we go to our new home which appears even dirtier than the preceding ones. In the refectory some women, crowded together, fight noisily. We go back to the *Blockowa* to obtain soup and a bed. We are received with blows. Determined to get away from this, we enter the dormitory on our own. It is foul and the cold hits us immediately on entering. All the window-panes are missing. Sometimes they are replaced with cartons but often the window is gaping and nothing prevents the freezing north wind from penetrating inside. A desperate Suzanne rejoins us. Her searching has proven pointless. After examining the dormitory in detail, we must surrender to the obvious. There are only several free beds near the windows and they don't even have mattresses. Moreover in our rapid inspection of the dormitory, we can report that the majority of the beds were smashed, ripped open mattresses hanging lamentably from the third level onto the lower level.

Andrée, Anna and Françoise succeeded in getting settled while Isabelle and Suzanne looked for a mattress on a broken bed. I was busy seeing if I could find some places farther from the windows. At first I noticed an immobile form on a bed. She is alone. This could be a good deal for Suzanne who is the most delicate.

—Madame, are you sleeping alone?

—Madame do you hear me?

—Madame?

Annoyed, a rough voice is heard from the neighboring bed. "Can't you see that she is dead? The *Blockowa* was already advised at noon; maybe she will have her removed by tomorrow evening."

This said my interlocutor turns over and falls back to sleep near the corpse. In the semi-obscurity of the dormitory, I did not notice her rigidity. I go to find the others; they have discovered a mattress. The three of us lower it from the third level and resign ourselves to take a bed near the windows.

It is terribly cold. We stretch out completely dressed without even taking off our shoes. We have only our soaking wet clothes to cover ourselves. In all our climbs, we have lost several things—a knife, my belt, our comb. It's a catastrophe. We spend a mostly sleepless night. Fortunately the next day a transport occurs in the block and we settle in a bed located at the center of the dorm.

⁂

Mme Melot is found. She is living in Block 28. She cries on the shoulder of her daughter, who regains the courage to console her mother. The poor woman is defenseless. The *Blockowa* has already beaten her. They have stolen her shoes. She had hidden her wedding ring in one of them. This loss drives her to despair. To lighten her anxiety, we suggest that she come to our block and wait for us every evening so we can dine together. But Suzanne is distraught. In the future, who will help her mother wash? Must she endure pushing and shoving to obtain her soup? Who will comfort her if she is sick in the night? During the long hours of roll call, she will no longer have anyone to support her. It is difficult to watch their despair.

I have decided to attempt a visit to Mickie who promises me that soon we will all be together in Block 15. I report this good news to my friends. They regain hope but our characters are embittered by all this misery. Even between Isabelle and I, there is no longer the beautiful harmony of our early days here. One of us is afflicted by cystitis; the other with dysentery. We disturb each other in the night. Isabelle never complains but my solicitude annoys her. The bond of blood makes us still worry about each other but the sufferings of daily life unceasingly divide us. The other day due to clumsiness, I let one of my shoes fall to the lower level. It was immediately stolen and I had to go to work with one bare foot. The ground was covered with snow. Isabelle pitied me but evidently I could have been more careful. I am beginning to feel worn out. To take my belongings down from the third level, I must always have recourse to her help. At work I can lift the tools only with difficulty, which gives her another worry.

She is here somewhat through my fault. The day of our departure from Romainville, the head of the French camp had told me that the Sonderfuhrer had almost decided to leave us in France. I only needed to take the initiative but I had energetically refused. All our old women were leaving and I hoped to be able to help them. Today with dread, I realize that I am only going to become a burden.

Like every day, we encounter the column of deported men on the road. While passing, we greet each other; "Bonjour la France!" The *Aufseherin* doesn't look at us. She jokes with the SS and laughs coarsely. She accompanies us for the first time. Short and stocky, she seems happy to be alive and walks along humming. Her good natured manner lets us hope for a nice day.

Having crossed the tracks, we start on the familiar little path that leads to the site and, after being recounted, we get ready to disperse towards the excavated holes. But an order makes the column stop. What is happening? The *Aufseherin* does a search. This has never happened on the work sites. Quickly we hide thread, knife etc. in our shoes but she looks at our clothes. Some have hidden a blanket under their dresses. She takes it from them while slapping them. All the raided objects lie on the ground. I am glad that Isabelle had not accompanied me: Being unwell, she had obtained a permit for consultation at the Infirmary. My turn arrives. The *Aufseherin* looks at my overalls, my pullover, my striped dress and rips it open. What is going to happen? I am wearing an SS shirt that I had bought several days ago. It is waterproof and warm. I had tried to tuck in the collar but she noticed it and her rage no longer had any limits. Insulting me in German, she lashed out at me punching me in the face numerous times. Stunned, immobile, I receive the blows, using all my will not to cry. My mouth bleeds profusely. She brutally rips off my clothes and I stay there stripped to the waist under the snow, which falls in large flakes. After awhile, she allows me to put my clothes back on. She takes away my infamous shirt and also my pullover, which does not bear the regulation cross. (Doctor don Zimmet had brought it to me from the train cars.)

Through an interpreter, I learn that I will go to the Bunker. We were all terrified of the Bunker. Before entering, we usually received 50 blows of the baton. Mlle Talet had told me that a doctor always assisted at the session. Nearly every time the victims in fact faint before the sentence has been fully executed. A nurse resuscitates them and they are hospitalized if their condition is alarming. Once restored, they received the remaining blows coming to them. We did not know much about the regime inside the Bunker but several had died there. For a month

Isabelle and I lived under the threat of this punishment; but undoubtedly, the *Aufseherin* had the habit of settling her accounts herself because I never heard of it again.

The cold intensifies. A thick layer of ice covers the snow. Often when we go past the large gate, the thermometer reads –28 degrees, –30 degrees Celsius (–18 degrees, –22 degrees Fahrenheit). To dig our holes, we must first break the ice with the aid of our picks. But the ground is frozen very deep and it is necessary to combine all our strength to drive in our tools. The *Aufseherinnen* are cold despite their fire; also they continually check the site so we saw and chop without respite. The temperature is so harsh that we no longer even try to hide to avoid working; our weakness is so great that too prolonged immobility could be fatal to us. Two times already Isabelle felt her heart failing. I rubbed it as best I could to bring it back to life. The little slice of bread that we carefully kept since the previous day had frozen in our bags. The soup now arrives only lukewarm. When we start work again after the noon break, the ground that we had such difficulty attacking is frozen again.

Suzanne changes each day. Two purplish pockets form under her eyes. She drags along with difficulty. Isabelle is losing weight terribly but, since I worry about her, she always replies that she feels very strong. As for me, I feel myself dying a little each day. I no longer have the strength to lift the pick to break the ice. From a distance Isabelle watches me and she takes hold of the heavy tool instead of me. I feel overcome with great happiness to have regained her sympathy.

⁂

The opaque night is silent. Then the heartrending siren snatches people from their peace and plunges them into anguish. The camp wakes up, stirs; some shadows circulate; little groups scattered at first become more and more numerous. Time passes; the crowd thickens; transforms into a turbulent human tide, which moves toward the Lagerstrasse despite darkness, cold, ice or snow. The women, pushed, shoved, lifted by the flood, gather their strength to force a passage to the place assigned to them. With great difficulty, the *Blockowas* and their aides try to line up their herds. Each prisoner engages in a cunning strategy to be placed neither at the first nor at the last row, most exposed to the wind, and seeks to be protected from the cold by a living wall. Little by little, order prevails. Impeccable rows are formed. The *Aufseherin* has not yet signaled. The wait is long. Behind the high black pines of the sandpits, dawn pierces the dark and lights up the sky. Occasionally an exhausted woman falls and a gap breaks the harmony of this immense parade.

The cold gains on us; the Polish women slap their feet against each other to warm themselves. The women talk. A French woman gives the day's menu to an attentive audience. Suzanne, turned slightly toward Isabelle, recites the mass; my sister responds to her. Placed behind her, I pray and, because I feel myself very close to the dead, I forget the living... In my mind, I make a pilgrimage into the cemeteries where my dead repose. I kneel before each grave. Ten Hail Marys for papa; ten others for my sister; ten again for my grandparents; I think of Gilbert's children: ten prayers on the flower decorated grave in Vannes, where Jean-Luc sleeps. Ten on that of Manuel in Spain and so I say my rosary and always I add a prayer for Philippe, who shares our fate in an unknown camp. The sun slowly rises; suddenly the murmurs cease, the dull silhouettes freeze at attention. The *Aufseherin* passes the rows and counts. It's roll call.

Denise left the Infirmary but it is painful to see her pathetic little face, her leaden complexion. Since I have the good fortune to have a little food supplement while working, I arrange to give her every day several small things that she comes to find in my block.

⁂

On returning from work Suzanne nearly faints. We have both been assigned to carry an empty pot. Isabelle is too far in front of us to be able to replace Suzanne for whom the pot is too heavy. After covering two kilometers, the poor unfortunate woman is exhausted. She moans. "I have no more strength. I am going to let go completely." Her poor thin face is tense with the effort. Only her teeth are visible, like a death's head.

I can't carry the pot alone. It's physically impossible. If she releases it, she will be beaten. Amicably I urge her a little. "Let's go Suzanne, have a little courage. We have nearly arrived. If you try, you will regain some strength." She bites her lips and says nothing but her whole being expresses suffering. Finally here is the turn which precedes a long stretch at the end of which is the main gate. Already the *Aufseherin* inspects the rows and the harsh voice utters *Zwei, drei, vier, links, links* (two, three, four, left left). The head of the line strikes up a German song. The stumbling column straightens up. Regardless of our fatigue, the entrance into the camp must be martial. In a cadenced rhythm, the wood soles strike the cobblestones of the road. Fortunately here is the main gate. Suzanne is completely exhausted.

The next day at the Infirmary she obtains an exemption from work for three days. I had to translate the reason reported on the paper: heart very weak, lesion of left ventricle. We decide not to tell this to her but we advise her to hide in the future in order not to work anymore.

I fell on the ice, my head made a big "crack" on hitting the ground. Half unconscious, I saw the whole column pass over me: nothing could make it stop and Isabelle herself had to continue en route. I have the impression I'll never be able to stand up again but the *Aufseherin* brings me back to life with great blows of the whip. Aching, bruised, not hearing her insults, I succeed, under the blows, in picking up the scattered wood of my bundle. At least I will not lose my soup.

⁂

Some parcels sent by families are distributed in the camp. Denise had one of them. Kindly she brings us a little paté and together we make a veritable feast. But the poor dear is so hungry that her supply is very quickly exhausted. Then Isabelle also has this good fortune. Since we are found, we understandably think that before long I will also receive one. But undoubtedly, we were not entitled to it and it was given to her by mistake because we never received another one. From this one, we made some little portions for Denise and our friends of the forest. It is not very big but nevertheless, it provides some joy for all. The distributions continue about twice a week. The Germans steal a good part of them; despite that we begin to see some sardines, some sugar circulate.... And the rule insists that it should always be the same ones who receive them. An inflexible law is established and nothing can make this supplement be shared since we are nearly all prisoners. It would be easier to make portions of fire. Some "collectives" form among the fortunate beneficiaries and very rare are those who divert the least thing to the most unfortunate.

Elsa, our *Kapo*, becomes more and more disagreeable. Now she makes us stand still for more than one hour before distributing the supplement. We wait in the cold or under the rain while she warms herself swallowing very warm soup. So as soon as we are served, we return quickly to the block greatly desiring to finally have shelter. One evening, I find myself near Denise. Despite myself, I am disgusted. I am happy to help her but she could at least make some effort. In the cold night, grumbling all the while, I return to Block 31. It is the time for soup. The distribution is made in disorder: the noise of arguments is deafening; two women standing on some chairs call the numbers of tables to be served first. With great difficulty, while struggling, I clear a path, pushed aside by those who brush against my snow-covered coat. Finally I notice Denise and all my anger vanishes at once. Hunched over, very pale, she stands near the stove. A dry cough shakes her continually. Eagerly she grabs three miserable potatoes that I bring her and excuses herself humbly. "I was so tired. I didn't have the strength to go up to 29."

Each evening we bring back from the forest several coals gleaned in the ashes of the previous day's fire. Many consider this to be a supreme remedy against dysentery. Besides, apart from a white powder, which intensifies the illness, the nurses don't distribute any other remedies. A large number of women are also stricken with cystitis, a very humiliating infirmity. In the night when we delouse our clothes by the pale light of the lamp in the lavatories, we see the sick rush in a long line toward the W.C. Dressed in simple night shirts from which their emaciated limbs stick out, often shorn, eyes haunted by a horrible dream, they walk silently like phantoms. These shades all seem to come directly from hell.

Nothing is decided about our transfer to Block 15. Fortunately we now live on the other side of the block which is much cleaner; but we are no more than nine French women lost among all the foreigners. Suzanne spends all her free time beside her mother but since she does not belong to this block, they often chase her away. Then the two of them take refuge with us on Suzanne's bed but very often Mme Melot is sent away.

⁂

Mlle Talet is sick. We have just learned of this and immediately return to 15 where, too tired after returning from work, we haven't had the strength to go for a week. Our poor friend has changed very much. Covered with her coat, she shivers on her bed. The next day, her companions, worried by her condition, convince her to go for the consultation at the Infirmary. She comes back sicker. The nurses responsible for inspecting her clothes discovered several lice on them, the invasion of vermin happening very quickly with the sick. After shaving her hair, they brutally plunged her in a bath of icy water and sent her back to her block stripped of all her woolens.

We find her in the evening standing near her bed. Thin in her striped dress, which floats around her poor body, the face quite small under her shaved head but the expression still radiant, she reminds us of martyrs. She doesn't complain and gently reassures: "I am tired but I am hanging on; if it's God's will, I will return." This revival of life is due only to a last surge of her energy. Vanquished, the next day she moves to the Infirmary. She dies there several days later without the aid of a priest, as she had so desired. Mlle Talet was loved by all. Affable and smiling, she always had a comforting word. Basically good, she never thought of herself and deprived herself for others with simplicity. She is one of the finest examples that we had. Block 15 is in mourning this day of December 14.

The infirmaries being overpopulated, a block not far from ours was reserved to accommodate the sick suspected of having typhus. Without hygiene, living in cramped overcrowding, they all develop typhus and die one after the other. Going to bread duty, we notice the morgue car near this block. A duty of prisoners is responsible for the dead. Grabbing them by arms and legs, they toss them into the cart. The naked bodies pile up on top of each other in fantastic poses. A number in violet ink at chest level recalls their identity. The cart moves off with some heads and legs dangling outside. Their eyes are wide open and staring.

Big Jeanne, our companion of the forest, felt sick. Put under observation at the quarantine block, she died there at the end of several days.

⁂

Nearly each day now, Binz, the *Ober-Aufseherin* is found on the Lagerstrasse, when the work columns pass. Young and pretty, she is one of the fiercest. As soon as she appears, a murmur spreads through the rows. "Watch out. There's Binz" Casually she passes near us. Some resounding lashes are heard and the bags flutter about the square. Too bad for those whose bags only contain some bread. Those are all lost forever.

⁂

Among our companions of the forest, many have left us. Some have fallen sick. Others worried by all the deaths resigned themselves to be employed at Siemens, the factory near the camp. Until now we had resisted, but I see Isabelle rapidly decline and I no longer have much strength myself.

After much thought, I announce my decision to Isabelle: we will also go to Siemens. We can no longer stand the severity of the winter season and at the factory we will at least be in a warm place. But she rebels: "If fate had designated us for this work, it would be different but we must never volunteer for a war factory!" I assume authority in my position of eldest. We must think of mama's sorrow if we don't return and take every advantage in our favor. Then we will do as the others and sabotage. She gives in but her face remains stubborn. I know that she only obeys in order not to leave me. That evening I go to find Mickie at the work bureau. As it happens, Siemens is hiring the next day. If we go to the place that she indicates to me, she will have us called to the office.

I announce the results of my visit to Isabelle; she chooses not to respond. All night I weigh the pros and cons of my resolution. It is evident that I am making the wisest decision; the forest with the snow, ice, bitter wind has become impossible. We hung on with all our strength but now we are exhausted.

⁂

The next morning we go to roll call equipped with all our possessions, our mess kits obtained at great difficulty suspended at our belts. I think of this new work that awaits us. Near me Isabelle doesn't say a word. The siren rings out. All that remains is for us to go to the place indicated by Mickie. Already the rows disperse. On our left I notice a lane without police and my fine resolutions suddenly collapse. Very quickly I grab Isabelle's arm. "What are we to do? Shall we hide?" Delighted, she agrees and we go down the lane with lowered heads. Our fate is decided. We continue to extract stumps from the hostile ground. I know it is crazy but at the last moment I could not volunteer to manufacture parts of V-1's.

Christmas approaches. Already the Germans bustle around and an immense pine is planted at the middle of the large square as a sign of celebration. But some said that a similar tree was also planted last year and they were made to pose in front in rows on Christmas day without receiving any food. They remained like that for the entire day. At Block 31, the prisoners make toys for the children with some pieces of fabric gleaned from the dressmaking workshops. They accomplish wonders.

In the forest, Elsa looks for some little firs to make a gift for some *Blockowa* friends. We also would like to have our fir but it is difficult for us to cut one without being seen. Two or three times we manage that but the SS always take them away and beat us when we pass the main gate. One evening Isabelle is punched on the nape of the neck, which makes her stumble for several meters.

⁂

December 24: We have finally succeeded in bringing in our little fir. Straight and green, its branches well spread, it now decorates our bed. In a corner of the refectory, barely concealed by a screen, the *Blockowa* has set up a table for her and her subordinates. The white table cloth, the green branches scattered here and there, the cake already placed in the middle, all contribute to give it a festive look.

Many of the Poles have received some parcels; several even have some letters. From their parcels, they take some garlands of silver and gold. All their beds are decorated and the dormitory loses its sordid aspect. Their clear voices strike up the Gloria. Christmas all over the world; great numbers pray and give thanks to God. But for us there is neither mass nor priest. To God of the humble, we offer our misery and our prayers. Little by little the songs fade away and some little Christmas eve meals are organized on the beds. The abundance of the parcels is revealed. Our companions spread out white bread and ham on improvised plates. In silence we eat our dry bread then lay down. Only the little fir still gives us some hope.

⁂

An old Polish woman could no longer stand this holiday far from her family. On this Christmas eve, she hangs herself at the back of the dorm.

⁂

December 25: We return to Block 15 to hear the mass that a prisoner reads in front of a humble crucifix. The day is spent in visits. We meet everywhere and exchange wishes of happiness. Then we go to see Lucienne, who is now in one of the little blocks of the Infirmary. In front of her window, we find Lotte quite joyful because she has just received a little parcel from Vienna. Always kind, she has reserved a part for each of us and, we contemplate our Christmas gift with pleasure—a little white bread, a piece of sausage and an apple all prettily wrapped up. We go down to the block so our friends can benefit from this holiday warmth because it is mostly a symbol for us. Mme Melot looks at her fragment of white bread with tears of joy.

Quite late in the evening Lotte, who did not want the least shadow to tarnish this fine day, gives us the news. The Germans have launched a counter offensive. They speak of new weapons and their radio resounds with their exploits.

⁂

While descending from my bed in the middle of the night, I dropped Lotte's fine comb. It's impossible to recover it. I'm dismayed. Andrée, who also used it, advises me not to lament; she will go to the market where she will certainly find another one. The "market" of Ravensbrück is held in the lane bordering blocks 29 and 31. A little contingent of Russians is permanently stationed there. As soon as the police appear, the sellers vanish ... to come back several moments later and pull from their bags stockings, sweaters and combs that they slyly present to us. Andrée returns victorious, followed by a seller. This person shows us the object of our desires, a superb comb made of horn with all its teeth, (Lotte's was chipped) but it's expensive—two rations of bread. After a rapid consultation, we decide. A collection is made among those who used the former one and the deal is done. I hasten to give Lotte the precious object that caused so much worry.

⁂

January 1 1945: Only a little relaxation marks this holiday. As on Christmas, the reveille sounds a little later: the work columns don't leave and the roll call, brief enough, only takes place in the afternoon. Greetings are exchanged in the course of visits in the block. The wishes are always the same: to soon see victory, to return to our families and friends. Unfortunately the news of the war in the German papers continues to be bad. The Wehrmacht boasts of victorious attacks. Despite our being accustomed to the propaganda, we feel that all is not going as well as we would hope. In our naivety, we had believed at the time of the Allied advance into France that all will go very quickly.

Towards January 12 when we had given up hoping for it, we learn of our posting to Block 15. This gives us immense joy. In the future, we will be near our friends in a block with only a few foreigners. Besides, many French from 31 are sent there as well. Denise will be near us and also Maine, that I often see lately. But Suzanne remains somber and anxious. Her mother has not received an order. Won't she join us as we had let her expect? I return to see Mickie but she appears quite reticent: Mme Melot holds a pink card and is consequently considered unsuitable. A project has developed for this category but she can not yet give me any details. Nevertheless, she promises me to use all her influence to have the poor woman included in Block 15 by classifying her with the knitters.

Our parcels are quickly made. Maine kindly brings Isabelle and I two superb nightshirts in pink cotton that she bought for us. Equipped with these treasures, we return to our new dwelling. Immediately we are assigned a bed, where the two of us lay down. A very clean sleeping bag covers the mattress with a blanket folded in four on top. For the first time since our arrival at Ravensbrück, we have the pleasure of taking off our day clothes and we don't tire of admiring ourselves in our long nightshirts. Denise lives in the row behind ours; she is delighted and we talk constantly. Suzanne has been settled below not far from us. Our friends are on the other side of the block. We will no longer have to cheat to visit them. We feel that we are with family. It's true the inhabitants of 15 don't appear to be enchanted by this intrusion in their domain. Their reaction is understandable because their block is well kept and they fear an invasion of vermin. But some measures are taken so that our clothes immediately go to be sterilized.

⁂

Suzanne has been shorn. We found her so one evening on returning from work; her poor mother is desolate but she herself keeps her sweet smile. Her bed companion has been to see the *Blockowa*. Suzanne takes a lot of care with her grooming but she no longer has the strength to struggle against the lice that always torment the weakest ones. So it has been decided that she will change beds; she must sleep completely at the back of the dormitory, near us. This evening, we take in Mme Jackson who comes back from Petit-Koënigsberg and does not yet have an appointed place; she speaks to us of the lamentable condition of the companions that she left there. Though the light has been dimmed for awhile, we continue to chat.

Suddenly in passing, she tells me of having seen Suzanne sitting on a stool at the Waschraum. This is incomprehensible since a bed had been assigned to her. Desiring to have a clear conscience, I descend laboriously from my perch. Suzanne is really there, seated in a corner, feet on the moist tiles. Resigned she tells me her misfortunes. Her new companions didn't want her; tomorrow she will explain this to the *Blockowa* but for tonight she prefers to sleep there without pointless arguments.

I am indignant. Moreover I fear for her fatigue in this uncomfortable position and the chilly morning air. With great difficulty, I persuade her to follow me and by groping along in the semi darkness, we arrive at the bed, which is reserved for her. I climb to the first level and try to negotiate with the woman stretched out across the bed but she pretends to sleep. Exasperated, I hit her with my fists and we come to blows. She insults me and defends herself. From the dormitory, impatient shouts are heard "Be quiet, peace." Firm in my sense of justice, I finally succeed in making her move and I help Suzanne go up.

When she has lain down, her bag under her head, I descend feeling calm. But I've barely taken several steps when I hear a terrible fracas. The large woman has thrown Suzanne down on the floor from the third level. The poor child gets up laboriously and, while crying, tries to collect the objects from her bag, which lie scattered on the ground. She loses half of them. The dorm wakes up and angry shouts are heard everywhere. In a murmur, Suzanne begs me, "Please don't force me to go back up ... I prefer to be tranquil down here." I must yield. It's too late to attempt a visit to the *Blockowa*; besides our bed is full and, even if a place remained, I would not succeed in getting Suzanne admitted by our neighbors. I bring her my coat and help her to settle down on two stools. Softly she wishes me good night. Before leaving the room, I check back a last time. Suzanne, head slightly bent, prays. Undoubtedly she offers this new suffering to God. That night I had great difficulty getting to sleep.

⁂

It's one punishment after another, without knowing the nature of our offenses. The blocks having roll call "pose" in their turn, which often prolongs this more than an hour. One Sunday morning especially, it's interminable. Someone is missing. For quite awhile, the *Aufseherin* counts us. Finally the missing woman is found. She was hidden under her bed. The punishment is general. This Sunday, we work all day and wait in vain for the noon soup.

⁂

Too many accumulated sufferings are the reason for our lowered resistance and soon I fall sick. At the Infirmary, they consent to issue me several consecutive exemptions from work. It's easy for me to rest on my bed all day because the available workers at Block 15 have permission to return to the dorm during work hours. Maine, who became table boss and who worries about my condition, brings me each day the supplemental soup to which her duties entitle her. I would be glad for this rest time if Isabelle were near me but she leaves me each morning and, desolate, I look at the snow that falls in large flakes. I imagine her on the site, struggling against the elements without a friendly look or a pleasant word to sustain her.

⁂

Infinitely tired, I return to Block 28. Mme Guéguen is sick and has asked for me. I find her with difficulty in the dirty half-dark dormitory. She no longer gets up other than for roll call and her eyes are bright with fever. She suffers much with acute dysentery but she has not had me come to tell me her troubles. She feels that her end approaches and she wants to entrust her will to me. Her treasure is still in her belt. She wants me to bring it back for her little Yvette. If she doesn't return, I can keep it for myself but at least it will not fall into the hands of the Germans. I am very sorry but I can't accept. My recollection of the scene at the site is still too vivid in my memory. Besides we're exposed to continual searches. If this money and these jewels were discovered it would be the Bunker, maybe worse. I can't see the usefulness of risking one's life for some wealth. So as not to disappoint her, I propose we bury her savings but she stubbornly refuses. She will entrust it to another.

However, she addresses another request to me. She knows that sometimes I could obtain some milk and she would very much like to drink a cup before dying. In fact at Ravensbrück, there exists a duty of "painters" responsible for redecorating the barracks. For this work they get a supplement of milk every day. When I was sick, I had bought some from them several times. As it happens since the poor woman barely eats, she still has a little reserve of bread and I promise to do the impossible to grant her wish. Already her near neighbors are indignant, "Milk! With her dysentery, it's a death sentence."

I let them talk but I am firmly resolved. I refused a raw radish to Mme Elbard and she was dead the next day. Mlle Vachon begged me to give her a glass of water and yet I did not respond to her request from fear of making her sicker. Without being a doctor, I can see that Mme Guéguen has only several days to life; she will have her milk. Going back to Block 15, I easily find some painters and obtain what I want. Returning to the sick woman, I give her a mug, full to the brim with the milk about which she dreamt. At first she contemplates it for a long time. It reminds her of Britanny, her farm, her life. Slowly she drinks it in little swallows then she lies down happy.

I was really blind. I should have noticed that Isabelle only returned to the forest so she could bring back every evening the supplement of margarine and sausage. Kindly she shares them with me. The two of us have the impression that this little addition will restore my strength. Now lying down near me, she in turn is burning with fever. I feel full of remorse and we decide that she will no longer go to work. Since my exemptions haven't been renewed, we hide in the morning in the column of sick women with Denise and Suzanne.

Suzanne has been somewhat rudely knocked down. She fell on an embankment of snow and, with arms spread-eagled, remains immobile while looking at us. Denise is nervously seized by an insane laugh. We help her to get up. As if a mechanism had again been activated, she resumes walking alongside us.

⁂

It's Sunday.... It snows. The so soft life at Block 15 is finished. We have just learned of our transfer to 27.

Each one gathers her possessions. There are many here who have received some parcels and they drag an accumulation of cartons around after them. For several hours we wait in front of 27 until the doors are opened. Noon arrives, the soup is not distributed and we are paralyzed. At the end of the afternoon, we are finally allowed access to the block. We rush inside but there is no discipline: the beds are taken by storm. Usually three must share a mattress. The dorm is dirty and very dark. Poor Irène lives on the ground floor; the mattress of the upper level is ripped open but she doesn't complain. Her smile only becomes a little sadder.

Lucienne, considered cured, has joined us; we settle at the refectory. Denise and Suzanne are near us. Towards 11 in the evening, the soup is distributed. Remaining too long in the pots, it has spoiled and smells sour. Nevertheless, we eat it.

⁂

Suzanne is disinterested in what happens around her and cries. They came to remove her mother. This same day when we were all busy with our transfer, an order upsets the camp. All the pink cards are leaving for Jugendlager. The Jugendlager belongs to Ravensbrück and was occupied previously by some young Germans. All communication was cut off between the two camps. As soon as this news reached her, Suzanne rushed to 28. Her mother was already preparing her belongings. The police soon arrived and the miserable column composed solely of old women and the sick started en route. One last time Mme Melot leans on the shoulder of her daughter; their faces are swollen with tears. In vain Suzanne begged them to let her undergo the same fate; she is refused this joy. Arriving at the main square, the two women separate after heartbreaking farewells.

On this evening of January 29, Mme Melot dies while going to the showers. God thus spares her the horrible fate reserved for her but we only learn this two months later. Suzanne, in anguish about the unknown place where her mother went without her, cries silently.

⁂

The alerts multiply; the discipline of the camp is all in chaos. The majority of the time it's very late in the evening when we go up to the kitchens to get soup. Slipping on the ice in the dark night, we bring back the heavy pots with difficulty. The roll call takes place in front of the block. A sort of indecisiveness reigns over everything. The Germans look for the "rabbits," who have taken advantage of this disorder to hide. Thus are labeled some young Polish women on whom the Germans had carried out some vivisection experiments. They occupied part of Block 32; the other side was reserved to the N/N (*Nacht und Nebel*). The most dreadful things were said about the "rabbits." Knowing some experiments had been planned, they hid. Found a short time later, they were operated on without anesthetic and several of them died. We met them sometimes in the streets of the camp. They were always young, often pretty and walked leaning on crutches.

From Lotte we learn of the return of the Petit-Kœnigsberg transport. She noticed our companions on the square and returned upset by their miserable appearance. They soon arrived at the interior of the camp. They were accommodated under a tent. Whatever the block, it was a palace compared to this tent. Some stakes had been planted between blocks 24 and 26, and a simple canvas had been spread out there. Some bricks replaced the parquet, latrine buckets took the place of toilets and there were very few beds. Some evacuees of Warsaw, some Gypsies and all sorts of Slavonic people lived there. Several women died there per day. The commander of the camp had this barracks, which had become a veritable tomb, destroyed at the time of the Allied advance. The day after their arrival, our companions come to visit us. All wear the mask of death on their faces. Little by little, they tell us their misfortunes, the very hard work had quickly defeated them and many had to be hospitalized.

Then one day just when they despaired of ever returning, the SS, the *Aufseherinnen* and even the commander fled the camp because some Russian dispatchers had signaled. There was a grand celebration. Starving, they rushed to the kitchen and to the warehouses. A general looting ensued and some little feasts were organized. Some French men, prisoners of war who worked in the vicinity, ventured up to the camp. One evening two of them stayed to dine with them.

The SS returned as they celebrated their liberation together. The spotted Russians were only scouts. The SS killed the two male prisoners point blank in front of their eyes. Then, still shooting, they attacked the warehouse. Trembling, some poor women hid behind some crates; they were soon discovered. With great lashes of the whip, the terrorized prisoners were reassembled and the long column set out to walk on the interminable road. The stragglers were beaten. Thus Nanouk, who was loved by all, died.

Indignant by the recital of all these sufferings, one of the women of the block rises, declaring, "I request ten rosaries for the extermination of these people;" and we all respond. In the face of such misery, we have forgotten the sweetness of forgiveness.

Suzanne becomes hopelessly apathetic. We are now responsible for taking turns to bring the soup to her or else she wouldn't eat. Long after ours is eaten, she still scrapes the bottom of her mess kit with her spoon as if she has to perform too great an effort to bring it to her mouth. Her shoes have been stolen; she left them under her bed, no longer having the strength to take them up with her. Maine fortunately lends her a pair of slippers. She falls repeatedly. In her last fall, she scraped her face and returned to the block, without even thinking of wiping off the blood on her wounds. We help her wash herself, but her face remains scraped, which renders it still more frightful to see. Yet she tries to go out every day to visit the Infirmary or different blocks, hoping to obtain some news of her mother.

⁂

Our friends from Petit-Koënigsberg are starving; no food has been distributed to them in the course of their long journey and they feel the effect of this deprivation. It is difficult for us to help them because we ourselves are very hungry; evening soup has been replaced by coffee and, for several days, the bread is divided into five portions. Lucienne, who benefits with Isabelle and I from the supplemental soup that Maine always provides me, gives them whatever she receives from a companion of the Infirmary. Divided up, this gives them only several spoonfuls each. The other day, Nicole and Anne fought over a bone.

⁂

After having taken special care of our appearance, Isabelle and I head towards the block of N/N to meet a companion from La Santé prison. Access is difficult because the *Blockowa* watches carefully so that no unknown person enters this block; all the more reason that *Schumtzstück* is rigorously expelled. Some steps behind us ... we turn around; it's Suzanne! Her unlaced shoes make her stumble; her tight coat is all torn and her face still quite swollen. It's cold and her nose has permanently formed a little bead without her noticing it. We recoil slightly despite ourselves. If she is with us, we will certainly be expelled from N/N. But Suzanne, conscious of her destitution, has still preserved her exquisite courtesy and humbly beseeches, "Permit me to follow you? I would never dare to enter alone!" We are monsters. Quickly we retrace our steps, surround her, and have her lean on us.

Without too much trouble, we succeed in entering. Suzanne has found the friend that she went to see and makes herself humble in a corner. Joining us in the block that evening, she is calm again. This friend, who is a nurse, assured her that the Jugendlager was a rest camp. Prettily located in the middle of pines, the air that is breathed there was very healthy ... the old women were restricted from any work and the roll call over there no longer existed. Suzanne fell asleep happy for the first time in quite a few evenings. I had always been told that there are some pious lies.

⁂

Christine, the Polish *Stubowa*, prepares to serve the soup. A pot has already been placed in front of her while she converses with a friend. From our beds, we watch the operations. The soup appears thick. Without looking at it, she calls "Table 6 French" It's us. Quickly we come down from our perches. While taking the first ladle, she notices the consistency of the liquid and corrects herself, "Table 2, Polish."

⁂

The German papers have been eliminated, but we learn from Lotte that the Russians are advancing. Various rumors begin to circulate; they speak of evacuation; many prepare their bags, the bare necessities. Well-informed persons say that there will be a shortage of bread; in fact it only arrives very late in the evening and it's already night when we go to get it. A little protection escort has been formed and always accompanies the duty. In the darkness, the starving women roam, ready to attack the stragglers of the column. Some loaves of bread have thus been stolen. The rations have been very reduced. The surveillance escort leaves, determined to report to the block what it discovers at any cost.

⁂

Transports continually take place towards some unknown destination and the women bring some blankets, which has never occurred before. Many work columns no longer go out.

The other day, in front of the kitchens, some women who were awaiting the soup were taken away in transport; they did not return to the block. Isabelle and I no longer dare to leave one another.

⁂

Suzanne has just been hospitalized; she is no more than a shadow of herself. The next day she has a nurse ask us for her belongings and her ration of bread. Several evenings later we try without success to reach her block of the Infirmary. The lane is carefully guarded and we can't get there.

We await the bread. It's late and the noon soup was very thin. To everyone's dismay, the *Blockowa* has just announced that bread might not be distributed this evening.

Near us, on the same row, Andrée takes care of a very sick friend as best she can. This woman barely eats anymore and Andrée asks me if it's possible for me to obtain a cup of milk.

Reluctantly, I descend from my bed. I don't know this woman and it's a real expedition to go to the back of the dorm where the painters sleep. However, I decide to set en route supplied with bread and an empty mug. As I had foreseen, the passage is congested. Continually jostled, I have a thousand difficulties in reaching my goal. One woman is making her bed. She finally deposits all her belongings in the aisle to be more comfortable. She only removes them and lets me pass after some arguing. Finally the painters corner ... I climb to the third level where they live; they still have what I want. I give them bread and they return my mug filled with milk.

Temptation seizes me when I see in my possession the beautiful white liquid. I am so hungry! If I drank only one swallow of it, it seems to me that I would feel better and no one would notice it. Moreover, I am inconvenienced by a stranger; ordinarily all those who agree to serve as intermediaries take a little commission. Will I drink ... or won't I drink? I still hesitate; to be in accord with my conscience, I finally make a decision; if the passage is open, I will not touch it but, if it's congested, I will take a very small swallow. Chances are in my favor because there is always heavy traffic in the dorm. I have only one fixed idea—milk. I already seem to taste it. Cautiously I descend to the ground and return. The passage is open up to the refectory! I carry intact the mug of milk to the sick woman.

⁂

February 7 —We learn that Suzanne has just died.

⁂

Some other women have just arrived at the block. They ask us to squeeze tighter together in our beds. In the row behind ours, several sleep alone, in any case no more than two. But they have said nothing...disorder is great and control difficult. The new arrivals slept in the refectory on some stools.

⁂

Nicole, Anne, the sisters Schuppe and Grüner and many survivors of Petit-Koënigsberg have been hospitalized. A doctor told us that she gives them no more than a few days to live.

While climbing back up into my bed, I break down at the second level. My large shoes in my hand, it was impossible to move and I had the impression that my heart was going to stop. Isabelle shouted at me harshly, "Well why don't you come up, you're in the way." A last effort and I collapse on the bed. I'm shocked, "Isabelle you are too hard!" But the dear girl gently apologized while helping me to lay down. "I had to do it, I thought that you were going to fall!"

Behind us, Hélène, the prostitute, eats some lovely slices of roast. She stole some coal that she brought back to a *Blockowa*, who rewarded her by giving her a beautiful scarf that was coveted by a kitchen girl. Soon Christine announces that undoubtedly the bread won't be distributed until tomorrow while nearby Hélène is heartily eating the succulent slices. Isabelle murmurs, "We won't return."

February 13: The whole block has just received the order to go out into the lane; several try to hide under the beds but the police chase after them, whips striking everywhere. We also try to hide but it's soon necessary to give up and here we are outside with the whole crowd. The ends of the lanes are closely guarded. Clinging to the door of the block, Denise cries. As she is often sick, maybe they will let her go back. But if we leave, what will become of her. We are unaware of the fate reserved for us and we can't advise her... She finally decides and approaches us. Here is the cattle merchant accompanied by an officer so it concerns a transport. He chooses us by rows of 5 without even looking at us. No one is eliminated; the knitters also leave...it's inexplicable. At a distance Mme Bernard waves to me in friend-

by hangars, soon crosses an immense plain. We are right out on the airfield. Already some prisoner duties with shovels on shoulders cross our path. This is an enigma for us; if we came here to work, why did we leave Ravensbrück, and especially why have we taken along the knitters? Our surprise is highest when we learn that the little camp of Rechlin where we have come is located only 40 km. from Ravensbrück. Even the most optimistic can no longer believe this is a flight from the Russian advance.

We walk for a long time on the monotonous road; finally the first sheds of the camp appear before our eyes. This is quite small and surrounded with simple barbed wire.

The personnel all bustle around looking busy with this unexpected crowd. They bring us the water that we clamored for loudly. We drink gluttonously and the bowls pass from hand to hand.

The blocks where we are taken are divided into little rooms with a wide corridor separating them. The washraums and W.C. are at the far end. We take possession of the room that we have been assigned. Fortunately only French women occupy our room. Despite its limited dimensions, we must lodge 70 persons there. Already some of our companions arrive well informed. Rechlin is infinitely preferable to Ravensbrück. The commander has been shocked by the sinister appearance of his new lodgers and, due to his concern, we will be well fed and well dressed. In short, it's a holiday.

Rechlin

February 14 – April 13, 1945

The soup, which is distributed to us this day of our arrival, seems to us in fact thicker. Here we have two roll calls: one around 5 a.m., the other at the end of the day. They are shorter than those in Ravensbrück. Between times we go back to our respective rooms and chat on our beds. These little rooms are much more agreeable than the big dorms and during the day, we make visits to some friends living not far from us. On the surface, this change promises to be beneficial to us. Though the pessimists argue that it's necessary to wait and see before rejoicing, we are resolved to profit at present.

⁂

This kind commander had undoubtedly read on our tired faces that it was essential to let us breathe a little. The time limit expired, he showed us how he intended to organize the camp. All at once, several of us were chosen for a duty that involved digging a trench. This duty did not go out alone but included knitters of whom some were even very elderly. Accustomed to live quietly in their blocks, it seemed impossible to them to be compelled to do such hard jobs. Those refusing were sent to Block 6 and start back towards Ravensbrück after several days, going also towards a riskier destiny.

Then the camp chief sounds the assembly and soon we were all in the courtyard. It's not an ordinary roll call. The officers attend and themselves designate the blocks that we must occupy in the future. Fortunately our group of five was not split up. Mme de Bernard was assigned to Block 1 not far from us at Block 2. But the great inconvenience of this shifting was that all nationalities again found themselves mixed together. This selection took several hours. Then the organization of the rooms required some time and finally we could think about resting. But the benevolent commander had not finished with us so soon. Towards midnight when sleep falls soundly on all beings, a clamor resounds again in the corridor. "Showers ... Showers." At first we don't move but the *Stubowa* leaps from her bed and orders us to get up.

Isabelle and I are not in agreement. She wants to bring all her clothes because she fears that they will be stolen in the bedroom during our absence; as for me, I think that there will be a check point at the showers and they will take all our possessions there. Finally each does what she judges preferable. Isabelle puts everything she owns on herself and I hide under my mattress what is most indispensable for going outside. After a crazy race in the night covering nearly 2 km, and a long wait, we enter a building. As I had foreseen, two *Aufseherin* inspect us. Isabelle loses the warm lining of her coat and her knitted belt (two items stolen at the boxcars). However, she keeps her pullover that she has taken the precaution of hiding in one of her coat sleeves. I pass without harm, my sweater being hidden in an identical manner.

Our clothes are piled in a heap in a corner and we enter the actual shower room. The commander, really conscientious, attends in the company of a non-commissioned officer. The water is slightly lukewarm; to soap ourselves we take a hand full of the detergent in a box. We receive an order to wash our hair. In essence, the commander stays there. A whistle blow and the holiday is finished. We can dress again but we aren't given a towel and dripping water oozes through our dresses and coats. Again in the freezing night, we wait a long time because the contingent of women that followed us must return at the same time as us. We shiver and our drenched hair drips on our necks. The wait seems interminable. Finally the others arrive and we nearly run to get back. The camp ... the block, our room!

On lifting up my mattress, I notice that one of my parcels has been stolen. So we were both right.

How foolish those who imagined Rechlin as a rest camp.

The day following this memorable night immediately after the roll call, a *Kapo* began to inspect the rows. With the end of her baton, she designated those that she wished to take. The five of us are chosen and we can only follow. The road that we take passes through the airfield; this seems to us quite extensive because we walk a very long time. Numerous planes are landing. The column stops; around us some military offices, some kitchens, a continual coming and going of pilots between the shelters. We are in the center of the camp. We look around us curiously but very quickly the *Kapo* calls us back to reality. A chain is formed and one by one the shovels taken out of a storeroom circulate.

Each one equipped with a tool, teams are formed. I stay near Lucienne, but Isabelle and two others are taken in another direction. While our friends walk towards the inside of the camp, we resume our walk. After a short path, we reach the work site. A plateau that nothing shelters from the icy wind, blowing since morning, a clayish earth that we need to dig up to make an excavation destined to accommodate a plane, this is the place where we are going to spend several hours. The SS and the pilots continually bustle. They grab some shovels and forcefully throw away the earth to show us how we should use them to do a good job. The shovels penetrate with difficulty into the slimy earth and surveillance is tight. Next to me, Lucienne digs. It's her first hard work since leaving the Infirmary and I ask with concern how she endures it.

Time passes. Accustomed to the outdoors life, I can see according to the position of the sun that noon is not far off. Faced with the prospect of a break, the two of us take heart. A roar of the siren soon proves me right. Already we put down our shovels but the SS rushes up, "Los ... Los." ["Go ... Go."] But the break, the soup? Oh well, at Rechlin the rules are simply not the same as at Ravensbrück. The soup is served on returning to the camp around 4:30. The work day is carried out without a break. Near us the SS heartily eat the contents of their steaming mess kits.

At whatever cost, it's necessary to overcome this disappointment, not to think about it anymore. Both of us are mediocre cooks; the topic of recipes is beyond us. It would also be better not to recall those who are absent. The conversation soon turns to travel. By chance I recall the Gulf of Morbihan, the boats, the Isle of Monks. Together we walk over the moors, the little shady paths. The thatched cottages of sailors seem very near to us with their bright colored shutters and their flowery little gardens. Lucienne is filled with enthusiasm; she wants to buy a house there (The money question doesn't interest us; she will resolve it later). I search in my memory, try to remember; a villa appears promising in my mind. I describe it but she doesn't let herself be tempted, the number of bedrooms is insufficient.

Finally I imagine one whose description charms her, very spacious with sunny rooms and a terrace that overlooks the gulf; on one side there's a view over the verdant shores of Arradon; on the other one finds the island of Arz with a desert-like appearance. In front [are] some islands. Lucienne is delighted; her choice is made.

Now it's a matter of furnishing her new property. For the large downstairs room, we think about some Breton sideboards in dark wood; some luminous curtains will give light. In the bedrooms, some light colored furniture, some bright colored cretonne fabrics. It would be fun to have a housewarming before living there. Christmas evening would be exactly right. Lucienne speaks to me of friends that she will invite, tells me a word about each; carefully we choose our dresses, then the main agenda -the menu! We bring the same attention to its preparation

The wind has not stopped blowing. The earth is also still slimy but time has passed. A whistle blow, the shovels to clean and the work day is finished. Now we can think about returning and about the soup. In the course of the following days, we pursue our dream tirelessly. Some modifications soon prove necessary. I remembered in particular that the chimneys of the villas on the Island of Monks were in general very bad and that the stoves fired very poorly. Some changes are necessary to the menu, which includes only hot dishes. Then some new ideas spring up on the topic of embellishments ... each of the furnishings are meticulously chosen.

. . . .

At a rapid pace, we again take the path for camp: a hard walk in this plain with not one tree to give shelter from a biting wind.

Anxiously we watch for the sight of several shacks that we had noticed at about 500 meters from the fence. Finally here they are. We take heart. After a long wait, soup is served to us in the courtyard and we have barely swallowed it when the roll call sounds. Fortunately it doesn't last too long and joyfully we regain our room. Nearly immediately coffee, constituting the evening meal, is distributed. We think about washing but the water pipes are turned off. Gradually we realize that it's not possible to wash oneself at night.

⁂

The days follow each other in succession one much like another. The work sites are always located in the airfield, but they change every day. Our guards don't seem to have very consistent ideas: a trench, begun the previous day, is abandoned the next day. Some holes that were dug in the sand to build several blockhouses remain unfinished. It is evident that the Germans especially seek to keep us busy but the work is often very tiring.

Most of all we learn to dig large excavations. When they reach a great depth, it requires considerable effort to throw the sand up to the top. The weather is bad. As soon as the wind stops blowing, it starts to rain. The days seem even longer with this rain, which falls without respite on our bent backs. Impatiently every day we wait for the signal to return and anxiously watch for the shacks, which notify us that the camp is quite near.

⁂

Isabelle no longer leaves Jeannot, who doesn't complain though a dry cough shakes her constantly and she is old. For my part, I try to relieve Denise a little since she is no longer well.

⁂

The obstacles to washing help the vermin propagate. Many sleep soundly or don't have the courage to get up in the night. Never at Ravensbrück did we have as many lice.

⁂

We are still determined not to be separated from each other. Sometimes Maria, the main *Kapo*, wants two of us and not five. While the moment before we maneuvered to not be picked, we rush together when she chooses among us. With all her strength, she slaps those that she doesn't want. In trying to avoid her, the others have already been hit. She does not at all understand this coalition.

⁂

Lucienne and I, seated in a train coach in the company of two other French women, look at the enormous crates that surround us. They are quite similar to coffins and contain aerial torpedos; it's a matter of unloading them. This morning we have been separated from the others and taken to this new work. Our job is nice because we are sheltered but these crates, much larger than us and set tightly on one another, baffle us. The Russians bustle outside. We wait, not being in a hurry to work. A big SS devil climbs up near us, grabs a crate and throws it outside. This appears to be terribly heavy. We cry out in surprise, which he takes for admiration. Another crate follows the first. In the face of his satisfied expression, we repeat our praises. Proud of his strength, he empties the train coach by himself while, sitting in a corner, we utter cries of encouragement. And we return to the camp after having simply lined up some crates without hurrying ourselves too much. In short it's a good day.

⁂

February 22: Today is Saint Isabelle's day. In honor of this, we hope for a nice day, tranquil work and good soup. Unfortunately Gypsies accompany us. It's impossible to cheat by hiding at the bottom of the trench because they constantly inform on us. On returning, I express to Isabelle the hope that the evening will bring some compensation; it would be so good to celebrate her saint's day; maybe we will have a little piece of meat in our soup. I can already imagine it. Always prudent, she waits to see before rejoicing. Here's the camp ... as usual we await our daily bread in a neat line. The pots are brought; pleased, I point out the soup to Isabelle. She can't deny that today it is quite thick. The distribution is delayed more than customary; a little annoyed, we begin to lose patience. Suddenly the Gypsies, no longer able to restrain themselves, rush at the pots to serve themselves. In their haste, they push and shove overturning them and spilling all their contents on the dirty ground. Unconcerned by our cries of indignation, they rush with their mess kits and scrape the ashes. There's nothing left for us but to return to our room. The block presents an unusual appearance. During our absence, some new arrivals have taken all our beds.

Resigned, stomachs hollow, we lay down on the floor to spend the night there. Our belongings left under the straw mattresses have all been stolen. The beautiful nightshirts from Maine [are] lost! Fortunately thanks to the dark, Lucienne salvages a mess kit that the intruders have forgotten on the table. We have only two for three persons! Thus we celebrated Isabelle's saint's day that we had so wanted to make happy for her.

⁂

All settles down the next day when the sick and unfit were transferred to Block 6. Some others go to 3 and we can again find a bed.

⁂

The commander wishes to see some gardens around our blocks. Thus is born the "sod duty." In a meadow not far from the camp, some clumps of grass in the shape of cobblestones have been cut out. We must bring them back and deposit them near the dorms. Some women put in charge of this work line them up next to each other.

And without a break all day we go from camp to meadow, from meadow to camp. The clumps are heavy, much earth still adheres; sometimes it's necessary to take several of them. The same route, completed such a large number of times, seems interminable to us. Denise feels her head spin while we throw our clumps into the place reserved as a garden. She sits down for a moment. But it's necessary to set off again. With her long thin fingers, the poor thing scratches the ground which still sticks to her piece of grass so that it would not be so heavy. After two or three days, the grass of the first clumps is already all faded.

⁂

Only the alerts remind us that the war continues. Here we have neither newspapers nor news. Yet one of our friends has translated the writing in large white letters on the shacks of the airfield. "We will win the war. We must have confidence in our *Führer*." The pilots' morale needs to be lifted. We regain hope. Constantly during the night we hear the buzzing of planes.

⁂

Perched on our beds, we look at the panorama. The population of our block has just been doubled. All those from 3 came to live in our block. Tomorrow at dawn, a transport must take place and we are all designated.

In the rooms and in the corridor, the women are seated on the ground; there is not an inch of free space and it would be impossible to set a foot on the floor. In order to obey the civil defense regulations, the shutters are entirely closed. We are sweating profusely; the Gypsies have removed their rags and try to sleep more comfortably with bared chests. In this crowd, there are many elderly women. We are only two in our bed, Denise and I. It seems to me charitable to summon one of these poor women and permit her to sleep a little. Denise rebels. One less is not a big thing and tomorrow we will be exhausted for enduring the trip. She already feels so tired and would so much like to rest! I'm annoyed and order her to make a place. Finally she moves. I call a white-haired woman who is delighted to come up.

Below everyone is squawking. Constantly we must step over them to go to the back of the corridor and the overcrowding of all these sweating bodies is sickening. It is impossible for us to sleep but at least we float over this human carpet. I lay down with the satisfaction of having done my duty. I had treated poor little exhausted Denise so harshly this evening. When I think at times of that terrible night, it seems that I can still see these poor women packed together with their suffering expressions. Several among them had white hair. I had been proud indeed to assume the right to scold Denise. I really pushed her but did not think of giving up my own place for a minute.

Everything is changed! The transport is canceled and the women regain their respective blocks. The corridor of ours is clogged with waste, many of the women had given up walking over all these bodies in the middle of the night to go to the toilets. In the disorder of the room, I find a spoon and guard it carefully in case one of us loses hers.

⁂

The *Stubowa* doesn't like Denise undoubtedly because of her sickly appearance. The poor dear is obliged to change her room. She cries helplessly. Her distress upsets me and, after several days of hesitation, I decide to join her. Delighted, she quickly finds me a place in a bed. I sleep with a Polish woman, who keeps her shoes on while sleeping and her feet hit my face from time to time during the night.

⁂

In the night the alarms follow one after another. Certain runways of the airfield are quite near our commando. One day they told us that the greater the danger, the more the sequence of siren blasts repeats. At the period of our arrival we counted only 5 or 6 of them and they now often reach 18 or 20. Isabelle sleeps on the other side of the corridor with Jeannot. I worry that we would no longer be near one another if something happened. At times we meet in the night at the toilet. I observe with despair that she becomes thinner and thinner. She sees with anxiety that I am no more than a shadow of myself ... but we say nothing about this to each other.

Many of our companions are dead and we are all in pathetic condition.

The administration of the camp is entrusted to some Hungarian Jews. Having arrived some time before us, they seized all the command posts. They are in charge of the distribution of food and never, even in the worst days of Ravensbrück, were we treated so unfavorably. (When any group of people finds itself in such a desperate situation, they behave in this manner to benefit themselves.) The soup is distributed only when it has well settled. The clear liquid is then divided up parsimoniously and we watch them eat plates full of vegetables. Bread, sausage and white cheese (These last two items are given to us two times a week) all are reduced. The Germans had provided the minimum for us to live but we are starving on this diet. One day some Russians complain to the camp commander; the allocation of the food will then be done directly at the kitchens and will be more substantial. Unfortunately this change would take place only a short time before our evacuation and the majority would already be dead from hunger.

One month and a half of Rechlin rendered us all unrecognizable.

⁂

The road that we follow deviates from the airfield; after having covered around 2 km in the plain, we enter the forest, at first simple copses then the forest itself with its immense trees. We walk a long time, a very long time. The undergrowth thins and a superb lake appears before our eyes. A wooden bridge is suspended over it but it is so dilapidated that we cross it in teams. Under our pounding feet it trembles and we hardly feel reassured.

Happily we set foot on firm ground and, leaving the forest to our right, we move onto a long sandy path similar to those that border dunes near the sea. On each side are some meadows; at a distance I see a glimpse of a little farm with a roof of red tiles. Walking is difficult in all this sand. The path is narrow and the SS, undoubtedly fearing that we will hide in the bushes, forbid us to walk on the sides. In German, in Czech, in Polish shouts of "to the right" "to the left" ring out continually. Our guards walk on the embankment, pushing back with their batons those who dare to venture there in order to advance more easily. The sand enters our torn shoes. We now lift our feet only with much effort. Yet like a frightened herd chased by cowboys, we advance while bumping into each other. Again the forest, then a wide bare terrain where some trunks of young trees cut in lengths of 1 m or 1½ m are lined up according to size.

Halte (Stop)! For barely 10 minutes, we are permitted to rest and we drop onto the short grass. The authoritarian whistle makes us stand up quickly. Positioned behind the piles of wood, the SS distribute the trunks. We try to get those that are the least heavy. With difficulty we hoist them on our shoulders and, miserable little army with rifles of wood, we start moving again. Returning by the same route ... the long sandy path that we cover again with even more difficulty. The wind has come up and we no longer speak for fear of swallowing sand. The bridge, even empty, already trembles under the storm. Nevertheless we move onto it, clinging to our wood which doubles our weight so we are not blown over the edge. Underneath us the lake has become completely black and high waves disturb it. Finally the forest whose ancient trees protect us. Another break and then a non-stop march to the camp. We arrive there dead from fatigue, shoulders bruised, arms numb. Marila, the *Kapo*, announces that we have covered nearly 20 km.

During two consecutive weeks of alternating wind and calm, we return to the forest. Now after the lake, we have another break and Marila takes advantage of it to distribute the bread. We have the impression that to eat a simple piece of bread will restore our strength. The stops are always very short; yet I take advantage of it to lay down and immediately fall into a sort of torpor. The strident whistle wakes me and I start walking like the others. In front of the piles of wood, it's a veritable stampede. Sometimes the piece that they give us is so heavy that we can't manage to hoist it up to our shoulders. While the SS is busy continuing the distribution, we take the opportunity to exchange it without worrying about risking a beating. The benefit is worth the trouble since we must carry it for 10 km. Under this enormous load, many fall while walking, get up, fall again. One might imagine seeing an immense way of the cross. Every other time after leaving the forest, we take a shortcut. Each day we impatiently await the fateful turn: will we follow the main road? No! What luck! Already we know that the next day we will have to cover 2 more km. but we are so tired ... it matters little. We only want to live in the present moment.

⁂

Denise, near me at roll call, has smudges all over her face. In order not to offend her, I gently ask her to come with me to wash in a little while. Pleased, she thanks me. But the roll call drags on. After the stampede of returning to the block, I find her on her bed. She apologizes. "Not this evening. I no longer have the strength." I manage to pass a damp cloth over her little face.

Since quite some time, Denise no longer accompanies us to work: the *Stubowa* befriends her and permits her to stay in her bed. I myself have great difficulty to do the long route each day. Isabelle walks near me and gives me her arm as soon as we go away from the camp.

Cheerfully she makes plans for our return. She is certain of regaining her strength very quickly and then I will see how well she will take care of me with a delicious breakfast served in bed, and a snack at 10. Already she imagines menus; yet I know that she detests speaking of food as she suffers so much from hunger. In a little while, I change the conversation. We must immediately think about gifts that we will make for mama and our sisters for Christmas. Our choice turns to toiletry cases and we find an inexhaustible topic; we will fill them with trinkets, scarves, perfume, handkerchiefs, and belts. Isabelle talks and talks, hoping thus to prevent me from thinking about the interminable route. I listen to her in a dream, but I know that the idea of comforting me also helps her to think less about her own fatigue. My God how miserable we are!

⁂

I had just almost fallen asleep when Denise begins to cough. At first I really tried not to hear her but the heartrending cough has soon completely awakened me. It would maybe be good for her to drink a little water? But undoubtedly her dysentery would get worse? And I am especially aching and stiff! Another stronger coughing fit shakes her. I get up with difficulty, slip on my shoes and decide to go to the sinks. She drinks ravenously. While getting up on my perch, one of my shoes falls; I recover it with great difficulty in the dark. Some sleepers, abruptly awakened, insult me. The cough has stopped. I call softly, "Denise," but she has already gone back to sleep.

Some Russians have tried to escape while going to the forest; they had asked permission to hide behind the trees to satisfy an urgent need. Due to this, the evening roll call is very long. The unfortunates are found again but all the Russians are counted so they can be shorn.

Since then we are forbidden to separate from the column. The sick must exercise their needs during the stop on the bare terrain, watched by the sentinels. When we are constrained by the dysentery that devastates us, those with better health, thanks to the parcels that they have received at Ravensbrück, murmur disdainfully, "They must not have any modesty."

Alert! ... All the lights are extinguished. Already airplanes are heard. In the dark corridor, some shouts ring out. A woman gets lost going to the toilets; too sick to wait, she dirties the corridor. The Russian guard, furious, beats her and the wretched woman cries out. Raised up on my elbow, I listen. It's a Frenchwoman, but her voice is unfamiliar to me. I turn over on my other side and soon go back to sleep. The next day this woman is so sick that they move her to the Infirmary. She dies there two days later. Undoubtedly they could not have saved her but the beating finished her. Yet why were her two cousins, living in the same room, not upset?

Equipped by a dim lantern, the *Blockälteste* calls the numbers written on the list that she holds in her hand. Arranged in long lines in the dark, we listen closely. Our roll numbers are said in German. 35,000 it's Denise's series. She does not delay in leaving the row and hastens to return 40,000 ... 50,000 ... 57,000 Attention! Our turn comes, 57,908 that's me. Isabelle should have preceded me but undoubtedly there was an inversion of our two names. Arriving on the last step at the stairs accessing the block, I turn around. Someone unfamiliar follows me. Already worried, I enter the bedroom to wait. The women arrive one after another. Here's Lucienne; she's 72,000. But what became of Isabelle? Crazy with anxiety, I rush toward the exit. A policewoman, implacable, pushes me back and closes the door of the block. I return to the room and sit on a bed. In turn, the women enter; their numbers follow each other normally 80,000 ... 90,000 ... 100,000.

Where have they taken Isabelle? I would like to follow her but I can do nothing, not even call her. In despair I think of Suzanne the day when they took her mother away from her. Everyone talks, commenting on this unusual roll call. I hear nothing and have only one thought; if Isabelle does not return tonight, I am going to die here on this bed! The women begin to lie down;

life continues. The door, closed for some time, suddenly opens. It's her! The poor dear is in shock. She was also worried. They had simply forgotten her number!

⁂

Thus go the days. A sort of stupor overcomes us. We haven't any news about the war and we are overcome by hunger and fatigue. During distributions of soup or bread, we wait in rows behind one another. At a glance, the thickest broth, the biggest morsels are assessed and the starving wretches push and shove and sometimes fight to benefit from them. We are determined not to become savages but sometimes, despite ourselves, an envious glance slips toward a privileged companion. Many gather some dandelions on their work site but there are none in the forest. Isabelle imitating the Polish women has tried to eat some nettles. Undoubtedly she didn't know how to take them because her throat stings her terribly.

The allocations of bread are so badly done that the two of us decide to equalize our portions. Having been wronged the first three days, I accept the little slice that Isabelle gives me; but when I am the luckiest, she stubbornly refuses to receive the portion that's due her. Yet she also becomes so thin and so pale!

Exasperated by the suffering, we summon our last strength to defend ourselves. I struck the Russian woman in the lavatory right in the face with my mess kit; she persisted in wanting to delouse me naked in a draft after returning exhausted from work. I wanted so much to rest! The shock made her stumble. Surprised and dazed, she let me leave.

But several days later as I brought a fistful of dandelions to Mme de Bernard, the sick Polish woman on the third level, bothered undoubtedly by our conversation, let fly a formidable kick to my head with her hobnailed shoe. My only hairpin twisted on my skull and I fainted at the foot of the bed.

⁂

Pierrette of Block 6 came to borrow my comb until tomorrow. I am struck by her staring expression. She died that night.

⁂

Immobile in the freezing dawn, we still shiver at roll call; yet the weather turns sunny and the forest begins to smell like spring.

The SS sing while walking under the trees and the *Kapos* have put on their light short-sleeved blouses; they run along the slopes, Carrying snacks wrapped in fresh white paper. They laugh as if they were going to some joyful picnic. We follow ... our bruised feet stumble over the roots but, despite everything, the forest seems very beautiful and the lake is quite blue. The sun is already high in the sky when we reach the heaps of wood. The trunks are now so big that two must carry them, one small with one large matters little, and the ill-matched couples collide on the narrow paths. “Los Los” [“Go Go”]. It’s warm, the SS are thirsty; the herd advances with difficulty, the sand enters our dry throats and the warmth clings to our bodies, coats and woolens. The lice, revived and overexcited, dance a sarabande in our clothes. The *Kapos* all fresh continue to skip along the slopes. Exhausted, covered with sweat and dust, we arrive at camp. But we already know that dawn will still be cold tomorrow morning and we won’t have the courage to leave our coats.

Unexpected luck that we all three had a little piece of meat in our soup. It’s necessary that Denise share this good fortune. Very quickly, so as not to be too tempted, I return to the block after having eaten half of mine. On the way, I imagine the dear child’s delighted look, finally my room ... the bed ... it’s empty! Where is Denise? Every day it’s customary for her to watch and wait for me. Upset I question my neighbors. The *Stubowa* disdainfully informs me that, during work, there was a raid in the blocks. Denise was taken to Block 6, the area for the sick. It's impossible to see her this evening. Devastated, stupefied, I eat my little piece of meat.

⁂

A pitch black oppressive night envelops the room. I have just finished washing and, feeling my way, make an effort to regain the bed that I share with Lucienne since the departure of Denise. A shadow rummages under the mattress. I know that Lucienne carefully keeps the ring entrusted to her by Nicole in her bag. The jewel is hidden in a tube of toothpaste. The previous day everything had been stolen from her; by a miracle after having searched all the beds, we had recovered the bag, empty of bread, but still containing the precious tube.

And at this moment, someone searches under the straw mattress. I grab the arm of the shadow, "Thief let go of that." With all my strength, I silently keep a tight grip and hear a murmured response, "Let go, it's Lucienne! If such coming and going in the night continues, we are going to fight our own shadows.

⁂

We have succeeded in reaching Block 6. Poor little Denise is there, lying down on the ground on a meager straw mattress. Under the enormous hangar, an entire population of pale and emaciated phantoms moves about restlessly and our little friend feels lost among these strangers. Our presence is pleasant for her but it is impossible to stay any longer. We promise to return. Her eyes still try to smile, though tears appear.

⁂

This morning I notice that, like Suzanne, I can no longer move quickly.

⁂

Leaning on the head of her bed, Isabelle cries. She is hungry. From a distance, I look at her, upset that I have no more bread. Near me, the Italian Margarita moans because she no longer has a spoon. I own two of them, having carefully protected the one found the day of the transport. What to do? I have never sold anything but Margarita is in good with the *Kapo*. She often receives supplementary soup and Isabelle is so hungry. I make my decision. The deal is quickly concluded. Without remorse, I contemplate with pleasure the half ration that I have just obtained and call Isabelle. In a few words, I explain the situation to her. Neither of us likes the Italian woman; we eat with good appetite. But the next day the spiteful SS harasses us to dig a trench. I have a fever and Isabelle mutters, "We shouldn't have to do that. From now on, we will give away but we will no longer sell anything."

The work column regains the camp with quickened pace. Lucienne is pleasantly surprised today. "It's amazing, I feel very well." At the same time, for no reason, she lost her equilibrium and fell flat. She hadn't enough strength then to stand up without our help.

The joyful voice of Odette burst into the room. Today the bread is whole, a two day ration. It's quite true. We marvel before such riches. Soon morale rises; if the Germans are feeding us better, undoubtedly they are afraid. It is a sign that the Allies are coming. These exchanges carry on and the feast begins, a little salt, some dandelion leaves, it's delicious. Pointless to keep reserves since we're having a new diet. But two days later, Odette comes back disappointed. Today the bread is in 10 pieces. Our stomachs, revived and spoiled, complain more than ever.

⁂

Lucienne is frightened by my sickly appearance and drags me to the Infirmary, temperature 35 degrees (95°F). The doctor warns me that it is dangerous to continue to work and praises the advantages of Block 6. I can't decide to leave Isabelle. If the long walks are too tiring for me, at least I will die by her side on the road.

⁂

We all three went to say good night to Denise. Feeling too tired to walk to her block, I sat down on the sidewalk while Isabelle went to find her. Here they are, leaning on each other. Our sick little friend, her face all mottled, is so frail that she lets herself be almost carried. Automatically I take a little leftover of bread from my bag. But my friend, seated near me, has seen my gesture and grabs my arm, "In the name of your mother, I forbid you to give it away. We can still hope to save you but poor Denise is lost!"

They approach us; the poor sick child is inconsolable at being separated from us. She silently cries on Isabelle's shoulder. Between sobs, she begs us to intercede in obtaining her return to our block. We would also love to have her near us, but it's impossible. With us it would be necessary to work and poor Denise doesn't even have strength to endure the roll call. I take her hand and gently, as with a baby that one wishes to console, I repeat to her what the doctor told me yesterday. Some repatriations are anticipated. The sick must be transferred to Ravensbrück where they will receive treatment in order to be able to stand the trip. They will be evacuated first.

Denise regains hope already, making some plans. I hear her in a dream, all my attention focused on the distance that separates me from my block. Would I have the strength to arrive there without falling?

⁂

The next day as we return from work, a truck loaded with women prepares to leave the courtyard. Denise is among them. The dear child noticed us and soon called to us. She was happy and smiling. We called to her, "You will see Lotte, Maine and Doctor Fresnel, who will cure you. See you soon in France. "Thank you, thank you, see you soon." Her little hand waves goodbye one final time and the heavy vehicle disappears in a turn of the road. Denise didn't return to France and no one ever found a trace of this truck.

⁂

Several of us are now no longer able to climb the three steps, which go to the block. To go up, we must raise one leg then the other with our hands. Despite that, like mechanical toys whose spring can snap moment to moment, each day we cover several kilometers.

I feel sick; still I don't want to call or disturb anyone. In the darkness, I get down from my bed but I don't have the strength to slip on my shoes. The walls of the corridor seem to come closer to me. Now and then I stop then start again. I would like some cool water. Arriving at the lavatories, I'm suddenly very sick; it seems to me that I'm going to die there alone. Defeated, I no longer resist. A hand rests on my shoulder. It's Lucienne. She helps me up gently.

—You're not well my little Maisie?

I am no longer alone! Already I feel better; leaning on her, I get back to my bed. I truly believe that that night she saved my life by her presence alone.

April 10 1945. This morning we dig a trench verging on the airfield. The nearby runway soon becomes unusually animated. Some trucks loaded with ammunition, vehicles of all types, planes, aircraft carriers continually crisscross it; all this equipment is stored not far from where we are.

No longer able to restrain myself, I call to Isabelle, "Turn around and look." But embittered, she replies simply, "They are crazy!" I have an idea and add regretfully, "If only we could warn someone ..." Time passes and the traffic continues. "Pre-alert. Pre-alert." The siren begins to howl. Automatically we raise our heads. The SS, worried, also look; the sky is clear and blue. They calm down, "*Los ... Los ... Arbeit; nicht arbeiten nicht essen.*" ["Go ... Go ... Work; don't work, don't eat.] Again the shovels sink into the ground.

"Alert ... alert." The siren no longer stops. The danger is imminent, our guards panic, "Hurry ... Hurry." We must even leave our tools. The hurriedly formed column sets off running in the direction of the nearby little woods; the buzzing of planes fills the air. But we must walk too fast. I allow the others to pass me. Marila turns around and calls me, "Hurry *grossen Alarm, Kaputt.*" [Big alarm, smashed."]

I can't run ... I'm exhausted. Isabelle, who already supports Jeannot sees me ready to fall. She grabs me and pulls me along; the mad race continues. We reach the first trees just in time. The bombs begin to fall. Our little wood is located in the middle of the fire zone; the projectiles explode on all sides, less than 100 meters from our shelter.

Instinctively we lay on the ground, which moves, and put our mess kits on our heads to protect ourselves. Above us the planes machinegun. The SS are pale with fear and the teeth of the *Aufseherinnen* chatter. We get very close together so as not to be separated from each other if we must die. In a loud and calm voice, I recite the rosary; Isabelle calmly responds to me. None of the prisoners think of being afraid; we are all filled with great joy. "They are there!" The odor of burning rises; through the trees, thick smoke appears. The racket lasts a long time then suddenly all is quiet. A young Russian woman ventures then to the edge of the wood. She comes back reading a wide-open leaflet. An SS pounces on her, takes it away and slaps her. But he did not see what she slipped in her boot.

We return to the block by roundabout paths. The slopes are strewn with paper. "Propaganda," snicker the SS. Our companions wait for us in the bedrooms. They are more dead than alive and thought we were all killed. The other Kommando did not return. A little Italian woman cries: "Where is my sister?" Our group is intact but we don't know what happened to others that went in the opposite direction.

All the water pipes are broken; impossible to wash. The wait passes anxiously; it gets very late.

Suddenly, the door opens; it's Monique. She is alone. In vain we question her about the others. She looks at us as if seeing us for the first time. Her coat is torn on the bottom and all burnt. In silence, she surveys the room and, suddenly immobilized in front of a bed, exclaims: "Odette ... Odette." We can't get another thing from her. She continues her crazed walking across the room.

Some noise in the corridor. It's the others. In fragmented sentences, they tell us about their escapade. Monique, Odette and a German prisoner had been designated to work in a barracks. As soon as the alarm signal was heard and while they themselves hid in a wood, the three others, accompanied by an *Aufseherin* and a German soldier, went to hide in a hole. All five piled up there on top of each other. Some bombs fell not far from this place destroying the barracks. Odette, the German prisoner and the soldier were killed instantly.

Odette! This morning she was still so alive! We are deeply upset. Monique, still feeling the effects of the trying shock, remains silent. In a corner the little Italian cries convulsively while hugging her sister.

⁂

Shaken by all these emotions, we want nothing more than to rest; but we're barely settled on our beds when the whistle blows. In the corridor, the *Stubowas* begin to yell. "It's roll call. It's roll call." It's late and we understand nothing; nevertheless, we are all obliged to leave. Outside the officers wait for us; the commander, the SS, all foam with anger. With great blows of the whip, they line us up and we set out for the airfield. We can't imagine that they intend to make us work at such an hour. Despite our fatigue, we are a little curious to see the condition of the camp. Our guards direct us precisely towards the corner where we were this morning; what a spectacle! Everywhere [there are] gaping holes, the runway with large potholes and shells of burning planes.

"Propaganda" said the SS! They are furious and, with strained shouts, organize the work. Bent over toward the ground for a long time, we pick up gravel scattered all over to throw it in the excavations caused by the bombs. All along the route, we discretely scatter it, hoping to render the runway unusable for an even longer time. It's necessary to continually bend, rise, bend again. Night falls and our silhouettes are barely distinct.

Their surveillance impaired, our guards decide to make us go back. We set off again at dawn the next day; the same unremitting work awaits us. It rained and we lie down in the mud as from time to time a bomb belatedly explodes.

Two entire days have been filled by this production line work and the coming day promises to be as laborious as the preceding ones. We hope to resume the habitual schedule but our hours of rest are counted. Being harassed without respite, we soon reach the supreme degree of exhaustion. The prisoners have been mobilized without exception; all the tools of the camp are used and some are very old. Badly attached to their handles, our shovels revolve continually; we barely have the strength to push them into the ground.

I look at Isabelle, Lucienne, Jeannot. ... No one speaks. Leaning on their spades, they seem no longer able to lift them. In the sun, their tense faces appear even more emaciated. The thin necks and arms allow veins to bulge like ropes. When the SS yells, we try to see the time on his wristwatch. It's necessary at least to hang on until noon... moments of last desperate energy. The return is finally announced. As soon as we arrive at the block, we drop heavily on our beds. Another order to leave! Haggard, broken down, we line up in the courtyard.

It's no longer a matter of work. Stunning news is spreading: "The camp is evacuated, we are returning to Ravensbrück!" And a rumor grows, "The French are exchanged, they are going to be repatriated." This news is so marvelous that at first we don't dare to believe it. However, our bags are searched. We are forbidden to bring clothes other than those we are wearing. Still wary with good reason, we persist in keeping our possessions. Seeing that, an SS, sardonic and mocking, yells at us: "Keep your place. If it means returning to my country, it wouldn't matter if I were to arrive there completely naked."

Could this then be true? Dazed, we hoisted ourselves up into the trucks that awaited us. Everyone talks; since the French have been selected, this information is certainly truthful. Behind us, some Russians are piling in other vehicles. Thank God!

With a screech of brakes, the truck stops and a last jolt makes us fall against one another. Through the holes of the tarpaulin that covers the vehicle, we notice the green main gate of Ravensbrück. Some *Aufseherinnen* wait for us and yell, thinking that we don't get down quickly enough. They wave their whips. When we enter into the camp, the SS guard is still there at his post.

We don't dare to believe in repatriation. On the main square, we wait a long time; then without going to the showers, we are admitted to the punishment block, whose occupants have left. This is abnormal and we regain a little hope.

⁂

Squeezed in the refectory, we sit down after a fashion with our knees under our chins. The room is semi-dark. Only a lamp on the table gives a little brightness and permits us to see the *Blockowa* busy enjoying some well-buttered slices of bread. We are hungry and ask to eat. She cruelly silences us, "Those who talk will be pointed out and won't leave." Suddenly she stands up. Her shadow, very large in the brightness from the lamp, looms over our entangled bodies. In an engaging voice, she asks:

—Who wants a ration of bread for a pack of cigarettes?

Our eyes follow the morsel that she holds at arm's length but we own nothing. She sits down again and in a harsh voice orders, "Silence."

⁂

April 14: Our column waits in front of the showers. Some discussions, hypotheses and projects have enlivened the morning. But the moment has arrived and, anxious, we no longer dare to speak. All the leaders soon approach, the commander, the chief doctor, the "cattle merchant" and two other officers. The inspection begins very quickly. From time to time an unfortunate woman is eliminated. We are at the center of the column and hear a vague rumor. "The shorn women won't leave." Egoistically we rejoice, the four of us have nothing to fear on that account. Then a new murmur is heard: "The doctor has just removed a sick woman." In the next breath, Isabelle beseeches me: "Raise your head. Look nonchalant." Our turn approaches. Still two rows; then one ... now it's our turn.

A quick glance at Jeannot, Lucienne and Isabelle; a brief order to "pass." I prepare to follow them but an iron hand descends on my shoulder. In vain, I force myself to smile indifferently but their jaws are clenched. Mercilessly, Pflaum and the doctor examine my ankles, a sharp knock under the chin lifts my head and reveals my ravaged, swollen face under the harsh sky and I am sent to the side.

To separate me from the others at the end! It's not possible.

I try to ignore them. Pflaum vigorously pushes me back. Isabelle felt an absence at her side; she turns, sees me and tries to follow me. An officer pushes her back with his fist. Pflaum passes on to inspect the next ones.

It's finished. One last time our eyes meet hopelessly; time to see her poor face streaming with tears, to call out, my throat tight, "Give maman a big kiss" and already the police woman pulls me away. Gloomy but resigned, I join my companions. We are only ten who have been eliminated. Without speaking, we cross the square. A familiar little silhouette passes us, Lotte. Surprised, she stops and stares at me a minute. Have I changed so much? But she recognizes me and approaches.

—It's you! Where are Isabelle and Lucienne? Where are you going?

—They are over there; we have been separated. I am sent to the Infirmary.

Lotte's face looks distraught. Don't go there no matter what. We spoke very quickly but her expression is such that I stop and turn around. In front of the showers, the column is only a dark mass. The officers turn their backs to us and continue their inspection.

Suddenly in a flash, I understand that there is still a chance for me to join Isabelle. A brief adieu to Lotte and slowly, not rushing for fear of being spotted, I cross the empty main square. The silhouettes become distinct; all my attention is concentrated on the massive backs of the officers. My God! Help me, don't let them turn around! A few more steps ... I'm saved. Silently, I slip between the inspected rows. No one reacts.

Finally I come behind the others and call softly: "Isabelle ... it's me." She turns around anxiously and looks at me, then cries and cries. Unable to speak, she grabs my arm and I resume my place in the row. The selection is finished; the entire column enters the shower room. Among those who had been eliminated,

4 or 5, including my friend Mme de Bernard, were sent to the blocks. The others, taken to the Infirmary, didn't return.

The shower room is like an aviary. Our friends from Ravensbrück look at us, upset. Koury admitted to me later that all those from Rechlin were frightening to see with their dark faces and their feverish, wild-eyed expressions. We tell them about our life at the commando; in their turn, they tell us about what has happened during our absence; the operation of the gas chamber, the frequent selections and the extermination of the poor women of Jugendlager.

Appalled, we listen to them recall their flight into the brush to escape the vigilant eye of Pflaum; the hiding places in the storerooms, the daily agony and the deaths of our dearest friends, Anne de Baufrémont, Nicole, the sisters Schuppe and Grüner, all the survivors of Petit-Kœnigsberg, dead! The superior of the Daughters of Compassion of Lyon, dead.

Irène, dead! Irène!

I am so sorrowful. I turn to see Koury but she still suffers too much to talk about her mother.

From the others, I learn of the horrible end of my old friend. Her white hair put her in special danger so Koury tirelessly used every ruse to hide her. She was designated for the gas chamber one day when her daughter was at the Infirmary; she left smiling. The good nun did not want to abandon her old friends, weak and helpless. To support them, she voluntarily climbed into the truck that took them to their deaths. It was Holy Friday!

We are distressed by all this news. No one knows if the extermination continues. We are seized by a heavy dread.

Yet our companions confirm that repatriation is possible because the Swiss have already led a convoy of French. Evening falls and we are all weary from this waiting. A Canadian parcel was distributed to each of them a few days before our arrival. Out of kindness, Koury and Danielle give us a few little things;

with pleasure, we nibble these unfamiliar treats, some cookies and some pieces of sugar. A policewoman enters and we listen with disappointment as she says that the departure is postponed until tomorrow. We must gather our belongings quickly and return to our respective blocks.

⁂

Lying in the bed that we two share with Lucienne, we try in vain to get some sleep. And because the shadow of Pflaum still seems to pursue us, Isabelle beseeches me, "Stretch out your legs. Think of tomorrow!" Trying not to awaken the others, we very quietly make some plans, but we are haunted by the fear of being separated again!

Then like sailors whose disabled boat seems ready to sink in the storm, we formulate some vows--at first, some pilgrimages, but this is not enough. Childishly we seek to achieve the highest possible degree of perfection. We will spend our lives devoted to others. We will never again argue. Each time that we pass a beggar, we will give alms. God, who knows the frailty of human resolutions, must indulgently contemplate us from heaven. On the other side of the bed, Lucienne says nothing. I know what she is thinking: —Being American, I will be eliminated and not leave with them.

⁂

To recall the agonies of the days that followed is still painful today. The day after this night when we had developed so many plans, we were all three eliminated from the convoy, Lucienne as an American, Isabelle and I by order from Berlin. And while some civilian clothes are distributed to our radiant companions, we were in the camp looking for a block to accommodate us.

Mme de Gontaut-Biron took pity on us and succeeded in having us admitted to Block 14, where she lived herself. This block was totally populated by Polish women. They were charming to us contrary to the attitude ordinarily adopted towards us by their fellow country-women. The *Blockowa* personally took the trouble to procure us some clean clothes and, moved by our weak condition, dispensed us from all work by her own authority. A Canadian parcel was immediately given to us. But what was all this beside the cruel disappointment of the morning. Isabelle had not begun to get over this and her sad face expressed such great suffering that I was very sorry for her.

And how to forget the anguished cry for help from two prisoners of the Bunker when we waited in front of the commander's office for our block assignment to be confirmed. Two male voices that seemed to emerge from the ground cried out to us, "What are they going to do to us? For two days, we haven't eaten. Do you think that the Germans intend to eliminate us? We operated the gas chamber." We could only give them some words of hope; the barred windows were too far off for us to be able to throw them any food. The certainty of departure had already lessened the past sufferings; now they crash down on us in all their cruel reality.

Thus a week passed without any particular event. Our companions had not left; the advance of the Russians had brought the front quite near and blocked roads delayed the Swedish Red Cross. At least this is what was said in camp and the departure might be decided any day. Our fatigued condition was such that we hardly left our beds. Lucienne and I had very weak hearts and Béatrix de Gontaut-Biron, who still went to the train cars, brought back to us each evening some phials of cardiazol (for heart disorders). She hid them from the search by putting them in the bottom of the noon soup. With sorrow, I saw Isabelle waste away more every day. Always very brave, she didn't complain but her good morale had disappeared. She can consume nearly nothing, suffering much pain in her throat. There was a bread shortage. The contents of our parcels supplemented quite a bit but our dysentery worsened from this rich food to which we were no longer accustomed. These last days were filled with anxiety. The *Aufseherinnen* let us surmise the Allied advance and we felt victory was quite near. Still we were in the greatest uncertainty as to the fate reserved for us.

⁂

April 22 1945 "All French women on the Lagerstrasse." It's the general departure; the order that we had no longer hoped for burst like a bomb. Hastily we collect our belongings and we come back to the gathering place. Lucienne follows us hoping that her nationality will not be checked. Mickie is there. She confirms to me that there will not be any elimination. The SS hurries; a great disorder seems to reign among them; the police ask us to tear off our numbers ourselves. So this time it's really true! Faces reflect the greatest expression of elation. One by one the names on the lists are called; Ours are really there. We rejoin the others who already head for the men's camp, evacuated that morning. A great sorrow darkens our joy; Lucienne stays! Mickie reassured me that the other nationalities would soon follow us but we would have so much liked to have her near us. Courageously smiling despite everything, she waves farewell to us from a distance.

⁂

In the little camp where we must spend the night, we quickly get organized and find a bed. The departure will take place at dawn and the police have assured us that the Red Cross coaches will already be waiting for us. Everyone's excitement is indescribable. I remember that this evening Chantal was our neighbor. She had left us two years earlier at Romainville and I found her in my bed without dreaming of asking her where she had been. Isabelle is full of hope, but she feels so tired that she quickly lies down. Her throat is still very sore. Fortunately I myself seem to have recovered some strength since she is sick. In order to relieve her a little, I return to the refectory to make some coffee for her; the Canadians had the happy idea of putting some in our parcels. The wood of the beds has been used to start a fire whose reddish glow alone lights the crowded room. Many women have decided not to go to bed; they sing.

I try to force a passage to the stove, pleading, "It's for a sick woman!" An ill-tempered woman turns and responds sharply, "Everyone here is sick." After a long wait, I finally take my turn. The fire is so intense that my water soon boils and I bring Isabelle the comforting coffee. After drinking it, she feels better. A dreamless sleep soon annihilates us!

Dawn already! Quickly all rise; again some break into songs. Rapidly the column goes through the gate of the little camp, walks to the Lagerstrasse and arrives on the main square. At a distance we can see the officers who attend the departure. Without stopping the convoy passes through the main gate. It's wonderful. We approach and it's possible for us to recognize the authorities. Isabelle murmurs with a sob, "They have lists!" Three or four women have been eliminated but still many remain! I force myself to reassure her. We are going to pass. But quite clearly our names are called! We leave the row with heads lowered! The column continues to file past. No one is interested in us.

Isabelle whispers to me:

—Let's place ourselves in the row; we no longer have our numbers, they can't recognize us.

Upset, I object:

—The convoy must be composed of a certain number of women; we will certainly pass, but maybe they will prevent the last two from leaving. We don't have the right to do this...Leave if you wish. . .

—If you stay, I'll stay too. ... We were mistaken.

Her pallor is frightening; I would rather die immediately than to see her suffer so.

The last rows pass ... Everyone left!

Fifteen of us had been eliminated; 13 French and 2 Polish women. The commander deigns to explain to us that he considers us honored hostages. He keeps us simply to permit us to travel in the most comfortable conditions. As proof of his solicitude, he immediately gives an order to send us a new parcel. His evident treachery disgusts us. To our great relief, he finally leaves and we return to our block. The sole joy of this sad day was to see Lucienne again.

⁂

Isabelle went to bed; she breathes with difficulty. Hoping thus to relieve her a little, I raise up the straw mattress with our shoes; yet she is suffocating. It's impossible for her to swallow any food. The gloomy hours pass. Persistently I see my brother Claude afflicted with diphtheria. Yet I would not dream of taking her to the Infirmary since she would not return from there.

Evening finally descends. Sadly I stretch out near her. Suddenly she speaks:

—Lotte saw the convoy depart while leaving the office. The completely white buses were decorated with flowers. A large Red Cross was painted on the roofs. The Swedes very carefully helped the sick to climb up. Maybe in a week, they will all be in France!

—But soon it will be our turn; very soon, we will see mama and the whole family again!

—Maybe!

A silence ... then she moans in a muffled voice:

—Lotte also told me this morning several didn't respond to the call of their names and the convoy left all the same!

I had also heard this, but I had so hoped that she would not learn of it now!

My God! My God! Have you no pity! Thus it is that in life, some sacrifices are pointless.

⁂

Water! I go to the lavatories to fill my mug there. On the ground in the muddy water, something shines. Automatically, I lower myself and collect the object -a medal! Well washed, the effigy appears very clear, "It's the miraculous Virgin."

I cry for the first time since my arrival in Germany. In her bed, Isabelle still suffocates. After helping her to drink, I give her the medal, "Keep this with you; you see, we don't have the right to despair." A little later, I try to speak to her again but she has fallen asleep.

⁂

The next day she drags herself to the morning roll call, which is fortunately very short. The *Aufseherinnen*, very agitated, run through the camp. While passing, one of them, announces to the *Blockowa*, "The Allies are at Berlin." Can we believe them? After a morning spent in anxiety, Isabelle went back to bed.

One of the hostages leaves for news. She returns a short while later and informs us of the conversation she had with an envoy of the commander, a German woman by the name of Mops. Through this intermediary, this man asked us how we would respond to the Allies about his treatment of the prisoners. Our friend had observed to this woman that a German officer should be responsible for his acts and that we would in no way excuse the treatment inflicted on our comrades. We agree with this noble response but Mme de Gontaut expressed all our thoughts in saying, "In my opinion, this smells like trouble. I think that it would be prudent for us to slip into the next convoy. I give you fair warning that, as for me, I have decided to follow the Polish women with Béatrix."

She speaks wisely and we decide to imitate her. Toward the end of the morning, a new transport is announced. Arriving on the Lagerstrasse, we notice that it is composed only of Jewish women. The venture is too risky; it would be better to wait awhile. Around three in the afternoon, the *Blockowa* informs us that the commander orders the hostages to meet in front of the showers. While hugging Lucienne, we promise her to advise the Swedes of her presence in the camp and that of the other Americans and English. ... If we leave? None of us betrays her fears, but we are ready for the worst. In front of the showers, two police women await us but they know nothing. A long time passes; tired, we sit on some cartons.

Finally two officers head toward us, one of them is Pflaum! Without saying anything about their intentions, they lead us toward the exit. *Our prisoner outfits have not been exchanged*!

Yet we go through the main gate with heads high. In silence behind our guards, we follow the road that borders the lake. At the left is the gas chamber and very far toward the right, we notice a crowd. At the fork, the interpreter with a sweeping gesture, points out the road on the right and announces to us, "You are free."

Our companions soon express exuberant joy. The two of us follow a little behind. To walk in the country for the first time in three years without guards seems to us unreal and nearly sacred. The crowd that we join soon resembles, in fact, an immense picnic. The buses are expected at any moment. To pass the time, the women settle on the edge of the road and devour the last provisions of their American parcels. Two *Aufseherinnen* walk up and down but they no longer show any authority. One approaches a group of us and recommends, "You will tell these gentlemen, won't you, that we have not been too nasty with you?"

All thirteen of us are seated on a little embankment, emptying our parcels like the others. Suddenly an immense clamor rings out from the groups; "There they are." Abandoning bags and parcels, all rush towards the road and already the first ones to arrive cheer the fine white truck, which is approaching. An officer descends from it; he is immediately surrounded, overwhelmed! Gesturing with his long arms, he calms this exuberance, and, after a long look at this miserable crowd, says simply, "Now you will never again be hungry." Other trucks arrive, but discerning that this officer is certainly the leader, each one tells him her misfortunes, the sufferings which she had witnessed.

With great difficulty, I force my passage up to him and beseech: "Monsieur, are you not also going to free the Americans and the English?" Surprised, he turns around. The commander of Ravensbrück assured him that only the Polish women and German nationals remained in the camp. The former should leave tomorrow. But I give him the names of my friends, the numbers of their blocks. As he writes this down, smiling, he promises me, "They will be returned to you." He could do nothing for Lotte because she is Viennese.

Lucienne, Mme Jackson and the others were in fact liberated the next day. As for Lotte, we learn later that she left in mid-battle. Kindly, the officers distribute cigarettes. Undoubtedly because suffering overcomes some people, a woman looking at these superb young men ecstatically exclaims, "Finally some real men!"

The evening falls; it's high time to leave. We pile up somehow in the trucks. Our liberators ask us to sustain one single night of travel in uncomfortable conditions; tomorrow we will be conveyed in buses but today we are too numerous for the number of buses and no one must remain on the road. The convoy sets off. Over there, the main gate of Ravensbrück fades away in the mist. Within the surrounding high walls, thousands of women still suffer and wait. Squeezed together, the majority sick, we endure as best we can this last ordeal which takes us to freedom.

⁂

April 25: Lübeck. The trucks stopped. Some fine buses already wait for us but, before getting in, we must be served soup. In disorderly groups, we go to the dining hall; the streets of the city are criss-crossed by columns of men in striped clothes. SS armed with submachine guns watch us. Anxiously our eyes search the rows trying to discover Philippe; sometimes fate is so great! But the closed and tense faces are unfamiliar to us. Later we learn that he was at Lübeck on this day, probably already embarked on one of the boats. In any case, if we had passed each other, we could not have recognized one another. The canteen, clean and hospitable is well arranged; warm thick soup steams in cooking pots but they don't allow the Red Cross ladies the time to serve us. There is a counter order. We must leave Lübeck very quickly. Hastily some delicious sandwiches are distributed. We climb in the superb buses without delay.

In the beautiful forest where we stop several hours later for lunch, we learn with astonishment that the truck behind us was just bombed; all the prisoners have been killed, the Swedish officers as well. The front was quite near and we now understand the rage shown by our drivers when they perceived that the German war vehicles followed us closely, hoping thus to be protected by the Red Cross. We are comfortably settled in magnificent buses whose large windows reveal to us the bombed towns. The sight of Kiel three-quarters destroyed brings exclamations of joy from us.

The border appears; we are in Denmark. A warm welcome from all the Danes, lunch in a cool room, at tables covered with very white tablecloths. Flowers, coffee, bread, milk! Our eyes look at everything with delight! The Gestapo accompanies us and our liberators hasten to see us safely in Sweden.

After several hours of rest, we leave these hospitable places to reach the station where a train is waiting. German soldiers move along the platforms. Despite that, the civilians surround us to pass out some treats. Several groups of people are standing around and all have the same look of astonishment when they see our miserable procession. I remember that day I wore a blue dress with red sleeves. My shoes had holes and were held on by some gray rags. Our legs, very thin with swollen ankles, gave us deformed silhouettes. The strongest climbed briskly into the train coaches but for the majority the little walk from the platform required a considerable effort. Some attentive employees hasten to gently offer their help. The train leaves the station amidst cheers and soon rolls across the magnificent Nordic countryside as yet unfamiliar to us. When we would so much like to submit to its charms in silence, a woman, proud of her erudition, analyzes in a shrill voice the stories of Selma Lagerlöf.

⁂

The Danish doctor that I had called tells me that Isabelle is now out of danger, but she has had diphtheria.

We cross Denmark, a wonderful country that we look at with tired eyes, first by train, then by boat, finally boarding at Copenhagen for the destination of Sweden. On the boat, the Gestapo regretfully decides to leave us. Malmö! No more Germans! Real freedom. Seated on our parcels, we hear them say that it's necessary to abandon our belongings for fear of contagion. This decision is wisest; yet due to old habits, several still try to hide a few little things. We rest for several hours on a boat anchored in the port; a concert is planned; groups of women chat.

Isabelle stretched out on a bench. She sleeps, her nose pinched and so pale that I am worried and lean over her; but she breathes!

We are taken to the showers in little contingents. Our car stops in front of a pastry shop; marveling, we admire some superb cakes. Standing up in the car, Mme de Gontaut-Biron exlcaims, "Who will trade me a cream cake for four Ravensbrück potatoes!" In the street, some civilians have gathered. Ignorant of where we come from, they look at us as terrified as if they saw ghosts.

⁂

All our old clothes have been abandoned at the showers. Refreshed, dressed in uniform blue tunics, we are put up in the Malmö Museum. This first night in Sweden passes gaily; some straw mattresses have been spread on the ground in some large rooms; several cut out curlers from their paper sheets.

Lucienne arrives the next day and our happiness is complete. We spend several days without worry, not yet suspecting that many carry in them the germs of terrible illnesses. Nothing can allay our voracious hunger but the Swedish doctors still wisely ration us, although to our great disappointment.

In some shops reserved for this purpose, new clothes are distributed to us. At leisure we can look on the shelves and we are delighted to choose our clothes with the greatest care. The mirrors of the museum are not large enough to reflect us so we admire each other. I notice with annoyance that my excessively swollen ankles no longer allow me to lace my shoes. I am distressed by my silhouette but abruptly, I think of Isabelle's anxious suggestion, "Stretch out your legs, think of tomorrow."

I still see Pflaum's face though nearly fifteen days have passed!

⁂

In the afternoon, the photographer arrives for the preparation of our identity cards. After carefully arranging our hair, we pose in front of the device. We want to send these photos to our families and wish to make a good impression. Therefore we force ourselves to smile. Fortunately these photos only reached us a long time after our return to France.

⁂

For several days, we have been allowed to eat normally; a canteen is opened at the museum. I see Isabelle, now restored, swallow fourteen enormous cream cakes one after the other. At a memorable dinner, we celebrate the liberation of the hostages. The menu has been carefully arranged, hors d'oeuvres, cutlets, sauteed potatoes, salad and dessert. Until this day, we had hardly been given any dairy products; so we greatly appreciate the taste of this food. I ask Mme de Gontaut seated at the other end of the table, "It's good, isn't it?" But too absorbed, she responds, "In a little while ... I'm eating." A superior officer of the Swedish navy questions us; we barely raise our heads! I'm afraid that, on this day, we have barely been polite; yet he looks at us, amused and smiles.

A large number of Polish women arrive at the museum. To make room, they decide to send us to Grimslö ... in a quarantine camp, a fortunate posting in the countryside. We burn with the desire to visit the surroundings but we are definitely prohibited from leaving the garden, with such danger of contagion not being isolated. Inhabitants of the little neighboring village offer to do some shopping for us. The food of the camp is delicious; moreover we have a canteen and numerous Swedes send us abundant parcels but we are insatiable. We will get visibly fat.

⁂

May 8, 1945: We have just learned of the victory. The civilians have shouted this news to us. Delirious with joy, we spend hours hanging around the radio and this much awaited day is celebrated by a superb dinner followed by songs. The two Swedes of the camp are invited; the room is all decorated.

But Ravensbrück has not finished with us. Several of our companions are dying in Swedish hospitals and this evening, I fall ill in turn. At first I don't want to admit it; my fever climbs to 41 (105°F) and Mme de Gontaut advises me to be prudent because she recognizes all the symptoms of typhus. I don't want to leave the camp and try to fight the illness by consuming a large number of aspirin tablets. At the end of three days, the fever doesn't lessen; my transfer to the hospital is decided. I immediately drift into a semi-conscious state; two times the clinic is changed without my noticing; in a dream, I see some masked nurses come and go. Obscurely I sense a presence near me. A nurse is there with a telegram in her hand. She reads: "Sparre telephones, Philippe excellent health, on the way to repatriation, letter follows with details. With tenderness, Isabelle." Philippe is saved! That's all that I understood; I know with certainty that he will return. Happy, I sink again into a half-torpor.

⁂

Days passed. I regain consciousness on a stretcher; I have again been transferred to another hospital. A blood transfusion brings me back to life. It's possible for me to stay sitting up in my bed. My beautiful room is all decorated with flowers.

⁂

May 28. A visit for me, it's Isabelle. She arrives all bright-eyed, joyful, superb! The poor dear is terribly worried for me. The quarantine is finished and in several days, she must leave for the home of Prince Wilhelm of Sweden where I will go to join her because my convalescence will soon begin. Together we speak of Philippe. The Red Cross has announced that he had left Neuengamme April 24. Maybe he is already with mama. Late in the evening, she leaves me full of hope. The little pain that I felt for several days behind my ear becomes intolerable.

⁂

May 30. The operation is finished, but the pain persists; it seems that my head is being ground. How can I suffer so! Lucienne comes to see me, then some Swedish friends. I like to feel their presence but I have difficulty recognizing them and my consciousness fades again. I sense that it's the end; no one wants to tell me the truth. Why don't they understand that death does not frighten me and that I simply wish to see Isabelle and a priest!

⁂

My room is full of doctors; they appear attentive but all hide my condition from me. As they leave the room, one of them, very tall, retraces his steps and softly tells me, "Ask for whatever you want, they will give it to you." The pleasure of hearing French spoken! Smiling kindly, Doctor Ask leaves my room.

⁂

June 6: The surgeon has not understood my question very well and off-handedly replied, "Yes" when I asked him if I am going to die. With this certainty, I call Doctor Ask to request that he phone Isabelle; I hope that there is still time. The doctor comes down immediately. Wanting to be set straight on this, I ask him point blank, "Doctor B has suggested that I'm going to die, but would this be today or tomorrow?" Surprised but emphatic, he replies briskly,

—You will be saved if they operate immediately; tomorrow it will be too late.

—Never... I don't want this! I suffered too much the first time and since then, I'm even sicker! Let me die in peace but have Isabelle come right away."

Doctor Ask listens, then, leaning his tall stature over me, tells me simply:

—Your mother is waiting for you.

A quarter of an hour later, I am again in the operating room. I wanted to do my best, but I feel certain of not waking up and of suffering much. Mentally I pray, "My God! to console Mama ... let Philippe return!"

⁂

A French Catholic missionary came to see me. He gave me extreme unction.

⁂

Saved! The doctors themselves had no more hope. In my great weakness, the memories return. I see Ravensbrück again, my dead friends ... Denise! It seems I hear her scream! Then the bridge of Rechlin splits open on the completely black lake, Isabelle disappears in the waves.... It's atrocious. Tirelessly Doctor Ask spends long visits with me so I don't lose my reason with all these morbid ideas. Patiently he listens to the story of these tragic months, then little by little, speaks to me of Sweden, of its customs, its poets; I regain a taste for life. Radiantly happy, I hold out to him my first letter from France. "You don't know my mother, read this." He glances at the last lines:

"Gilbert occupies a high post earned by his merits, Claude is very esteemed by his leaders and received numerous decorations. From some friends, I know that Philippe had been very good and very brave in his camp and you, my two precious daughters, you have been very brave also. I am very happy to have you as my children."

Five agonizing years are summarized in these few sentences.

⁂

Philippe has not yet returned; no other news of him has reached us since the message from the Red Cross and all the letters from France insistently ask us to make some inquiries. I write to all sides but I hit a wall. None of the replies mention his name. Pastor Hoffmann passes by the hospital and comes to visit me. As he must return to Lund where Jean Rousseau, Philippe's friend, is being treated, he promises me to question him and tell me the truth.

⁂

June 18. Lucienne and Isabelle have come to spend the day with me. In my little room, we have a victory celebration, which we would very much have liked to attend in France. The Swedes have sent me some flowers and flags. We spend a wonderful day.

⁂

I would be perfectly happy if there was not this uncertainty in the matter of Philippe. This is becoming an obsession. A Swiss civilian visits me. As he asks what would please me, I respond sincerely, "Could you not find my brother?" Sadly, he explains to me that he comes only to give me new clothes. In fact, while I was in a coma, my Polish companions, undoubtedly giving in to an old habit, had stolen my lovely outfits.

⁂

June 24: Pastor Hoffmann had word. He saw Jean Rousseau and two other friends of Philippe. All three have given the same information. Philippe left Neuengamme in the direction of Lübeck. He was then in good physical condition; but what became of this transport remains terribly confused. One part, which included Doctor Jackson and his son, was directed toward Lübeck; another took the road to Hamburg. Jean Rousseau hopes that Philippe went with this last contingent because the other was nearly completely decimated. Dr. Jackson died in the port of Lübeck but his son turns out to be among the rare survivors. And the pastor concluded: "We can only wait, pray to God and thank him for having given your brother such strength that it was a blessing for many of his friends." This letter upset me. Despite everything, I hang on to the hope that Philippe had been taken to Hamburg.

Summer begins in Sweden and the nights are wonderful, they only last a few hours. Flowers and green foliage everywhere. From my bed, I can see the lake. Some envoys from the French House of Repatriation pay a visit to the sick in the hospital. They confirm that the Allies have not let any news of occupied Germany get out. Prisoners return to France without warning. I let myself regain hope.

Several of our friends have already been repatriated but some return with a broken heart. On the day of her liberation, Lily de Rambuteau learned of the death of her husband in a concentration camp. Mme de Bernard, sick and treated in a hospital, knows nothing of her husband and worries. Michèle Facq sister of Madeleine Laurent tries vainly to have news of her husband deported in 1943.

A young French woman had been operated on the same day as I. On arriving at the hospital, she was able to write to her parents; the illness worsened and she died just when their replies, full of tenderness, were being sent back to her.

⁂

June 30. Splendid awakening; Doctor Börner has just informed me that I will be able to return to France in two weeks. The mail brings me a long letter from Lucienne, she sends me a copy of the letter written by Philippe Jackson to an uncle in Switzerland:

Here is our news; it is tragic. I ask you to pass this on to the rest of my family.

My father and I arrived at the Camp of Neuengamme in July 1944. We stayed there for nine months. We were able to survive this.

We had been evacuated in the direction of Lübeck and embarked in the bottom of the hold of a cargo ship, Thielbeck. It raised anchor an hour before the arrival of some English reconnaissance units. We made the trip up to the harbor of Neustadt in the Gulf of Lübeck. There we anchored. There were three steamers, the Thielbeck, (about 2,000 prisoners), the Cap-Arcona, (about 7,000) and the Athena (2,000). The morning of May third, the English, who, were nearby on the shore, ordered the ships to return to port, believing them loaded with troops and retreating German soldiers. The Athena returns. The others stay by order of the SS who are on board. At 3 in the afternoon after a warning, we were sunk. At first the Cap-Arcona, then the Thielbeck, on which I was.

The Cap-Arcona caught fire; our boat sank in 10 minutes. By luck I was on the deck and wasn't wounded by the projectiles. I waited for my father five minutes while the boat sank; not seeing him, I jumped into the sea. I was able to reach one of the lifeboats before the Germans knew that I was a prisoner. Later they only saved their boats and their soldiers and let the prisoners sink. The first 150 to arrive at the shore were shot by the SS and really I ought to have been as well.

One of the rare survivors saw my father about 100 m from the boat, floating on his back. He was already in dif-

ficulty. I did not find him among the survivors. I ask you to communicate this news to my aunt if she still lives. I think that my mother died in a concentration camp.

I was stunned by the tragic tone of this letter and the resignation with which this boy of 17, who just suffered such a shock, contemplates the death of his entire family.

This drama in which Philippe may have been involved appears to me in all its horror; but then, even though I ought to be filled with anguish, I consider all the opportunities he had to escape. There's no proof that he was not taken to Hamburg and, if he was at Lübeck, there was still a chance he embarked on the Athena that returned to the port. If fate assigned him to one of the boats that sank, he was a very good swimmer and could have regained the shore like Philippe Jackson. Against all probability, I feel reassured by these different suppositions and I am grateful to Lucienne to have passed on this letter to me.

⁂

With pleasure, I look at the mail scattered on my bed. Among numerous letters from France, a long letter from mama, always great happiness to reread her tender words. Then a letter from Matelot; I recognize her little writing and rejoice, her words amuse me because she always gives me all the news. I was not mistaken, here it is already:

You are going to be happy, dear Pierre came back, François of Romainville also, all the prisoners come back without having been able to write and inform so there is a wild crowd at the arrival of the trains. Each evening Hélène and I return to the station hoping to find our dear Philippe.

The news of my two friends' return fills me with joy. Then I try to imagine the station of Vannes, the smile of Madeleine, the slightly tense expression of Hélène watching for the travelers, the arrival of the train; Philippe descending, beaming, a sailor's bag on his back. Philippe descending from the train... the vision blurs. I see him again so sad standing in the mist the day of our departure from Compiègne. Wishing to recapture my reverie, I search the page and again read, "Every evening, Hélène and I return to the station..." and only then I understood that Philippe was dead. That same evening, I sent a telegram to a friend in Vannes, imploring him to make my sisters understand that they must no longer trouble themselves.

July 11, 1945. Isabelle is there. The expected time for my convalescence has passed; we are returning to France. I am delighted at the idea of seeing all my friends and my family but am sad to leave this hospital of Växjö, where I have been well treated.

We catch a plane at Stockholm; several prisoners go with us, all come from Neuengamme. Among them they speak of the tragedy of Lübeck. Men [are] piled in the holds, anxious over the fate reserved for them. Their terrifying wait during several days without hygiene and nearly without food in terrible overcrowding and suddenly the drama, the bombing, the rush of prisoners walking over each other to try to reach the deck; the first arrivals jumping into the water. Dr. Barreau knocked out by a falling rowboat, others machine-gunned, the moaning of the wounded, the despair of the men remaining on the burning boat.... Philippe!

Koury and Michèle Facq are also there. Several women accompany them but we don't know them. The plane takes off; raised on my stretcher, I look one last time at the forests and lakes of Sweden.

The nurse comes and goes among us; she announces: "We are flying over Germany!" Everyone rushes to the windows; faces suddenly harden. Koury lies down, a handkerchief at her eyes. She gently pushes away the assistant who approaches, believing her sick. Germany! She leaves her mother there. I guess that, distraught, she wants to hide her tears amidst the joy of others.

The Gulf of Lübeck! Those from Neuengamme look out with interest. I raise up also, blue water brilliantly sparking with sunlight, that's all. No one can see me; laying down again under the ceiling of the plane, I cry without restraint. Yet Isabelle has also thought about this last farewell and silently gets up and comes to hug me.

Several hours later, France's borders appear, then Bourget. The families are there, beaming and emotional. On descending from the plane, Michèle Facq learns that her husband died at Schirmeck.

⁂

Our family is late; we go to wait for them at the officer's room. Lying on my stretcher and a little dazed, I watch Isabelle, who paces in the room like a caged lion. The door opens. Gilbert enters first and hugs us, while forcing himself to control his emotion; behind him, Hélène and Jacqueline crying and unable to speak. Claude, who is also there, does not try to restrain his tears and sobs like a child. A little apart with her son in her arms, his young wife, who doesn't know us yet, looks at us. As we ride in the auto, I question Gilbert to know if he had some details regarding Philippe. At my request, his face tensed into an expression of suffering and near me Hélène murmurs, "Don't speak about it ... not now."

After a week of rest in Paris, we take the route to Brittany; the train rolls too slowly for our wishes and finally we arrive at Vannes in the evening. On the platform of the station, Mama, some cousins, and a crowd of people wait for us -all bring us flowers. Michèle, the little daughter of Philippe, clinging to mama's arm, repeats constantly, "Granny, tell me since my aunts have returned, is papa going to come back soon?" In the house full of flowers, we find Madeleine, sick again. It's one visit after another. We feel happy and a little dazed.

A very little girl with curly blond hair enters, accompanied by her nanny. She is so cute that I bend over her:

—Hello, my dear!

—Hello madame!

Timidly she puts her little hand in mine. Then an old Breton woman exclaims in surprise:

—But she's your niece, the second daughter of Monsieur Philippe.

It's Marion, born several days after our arrest. Already three years have passed!

⁂

On leaving Ravensbrück, I did not want to look back but I was not able to forget. The physical miseries have lessened, but Suzanne so frail and yet so valiant, Denise smiling brightly though close to tears, Nicole with a slightly fearful expression and all those that we have lost rise up suddenly in my memory, marked by the acuteness of their sufferings.

And as if to remind me that they have finally found peace, the shining faces of Irène, Mlle Talet and the good nun appear.

Would that their memory helps us to dispel all hatred and to understand that the sole joy in life resides in spreading happiness.

Arradon, August 1947

List of personal and surnames mentioned in this text

A

Agnès .... Agnès Von Boetzeler, maiden name de Beaufort. Deported August 15 1944. Returned. Repatriated by Sweden.
Her husband was deported on the same date, same train. Deceased

Andrée .... Andrée Levallois. Deported, hired on the wood column. Returned. Repatriated by Sweden.

Anna .... Anna Kervella. Deported, hired on the wood column. Returned. Repatriated by Sweden.

Anne .... Anne de Beaufrémont. Deported August 15, 1944, included in the Transport of Petit-Koënigsberg. Returned to Ravensbrück at the evacuation of the commando. Deceased.

Ask .... Doctor Ask, doctor at the hospital of Växjö, Sweden.

Audibert .... Mme Audibert, wife of General Audibert. Deported May 1944. Deceased.

B

Barreau .... Doctor Barreau. Deported to Neuengamme. Deceased in the shipwreck at Lübeck, May 3, 1945.

Béatrix......... See Gontaut-Biron.

Bernard .... Countess Anne-Marie de Bernard (called Mouse). Deported end of January 1944. Returned. Repatriated by Sweden.

Her husband Pierre de Bernard. Deported. Returned.

Börner .... Chief surgeon at the hospital of Växjö, Sweden.

Boulloch .... Mme Boulloch. Deported August 15 1944. Deceased.
Her husband and son. Deported. Deceased.

C

Claude .... My youngest brother, left Lorient for England June 18, 1940, officer of the First Division of the Free French.

D

Danielle . . . . Anise Girard (Mme Postel-Vinay), arrested in August 1942. Deported. Returned. Repatriated by Sweden.

Denise . . . . Denise Fournaise, 21 years old in the réseau "Libération-Nord" Deported in May 1944, included in the commando of Rechlin, left the commando in a truck March 30, 1945. Deceased.

Dixon . . . . Lucienne Dixon (called Jeff) of the réseau "C.N.D. Castille" arrested April 1 1942, liberated May 12 1942, arrested October 27 1942, liberated January 15 1943, arrested December 6, 1943. Deported August 15, 1944, included in the commandos of Torgaü and Rechlin. Returned. Repatriated by Sweden.

Don Zimmet . . . . Doctor don Zimmet (♀). Deported early 1944. Returned. Repatriated by Switzerland.

E

Elbard . . . . Mme Elbard (in her sixties). Deported August 15, 1944. Deceased.

Elsa (p. 15) . . . . . . German prisoner directing the work bureau.

Elsa (p. 35) . . . . . . German prisoner (kapo of the wood column).

F

Facq . . . . Mme Facq, born Michèle Laurent, in the réseau "C.N.D. Castille" (Confrérie de Notre Dame, Society of Our Lady); arrested June 10 1942. Deported April 27 1943. Returned. Repatriated by Sweden.

Her husband, Georges Facq (called Favreau) of the réseau "C.N.D." deported July 9, 1943. Deceased at Schirmeck camp.

Fournaise. . . . . . . Mme Fournaise, mother of Denise, of the réseau (Résistance cell) C.N.D "Libération-Nord;" arrested February 1 1944, liberated from Romainville by the Swedish consul and the French Red Cross August 19, 1944.

Wife of Lieutenant Colonel Fournaise of réseau "Libération Nord," regional chief of the Résistance in the West. Arrested February 1 1944. Died for France June 12, 1944.

François Louis (preface) . . . Réseau "C.N.D. Castille" arrested in September 1942. Deported to Neuengamme. Returned (survivor of the shipwreck at Lübeck).

Françoise . . . . Françoise Etève. Deported (selected for the wood column) Returned. Repatriated by Sweden.

Fresnel . . . . Doctor Fresnel (♀). Deported August 15 1944. Assigned to the Infirmary at Ravensbrück, saved the life of many friends thanks to her dedication. Returned. Repatriated by Switzerland.

G

Gilbert . . . . My oldest brother (Colonel Rémy), head of réseau "C.N.D"

Gontaut-Biron. . . Comtesse Anka de Gontaut-Biron, Deported in 1944. Returned. Repatriated by Sweden.

Béatrix de Gontaut-Biron (Countess of Toulouse-Lautrec) Deported in 1944. Returned. Repatriated by Sweden.

Germaine. . . . . . . Germaine Tillion, called Koury, daughter of Mme Tillion, called Irène (deceased). Deported October 1943. Returned. Repatriated by Sweden.

Grannie . . . . Name by which her grand-children called my mother.

Grüner . . . . Mme Grüner. Deported August 15, 1944, Torgaü Commando, then Petit-Koënigsberg. Returned to Ravensbrück at the evacuation of this commando. Deceased.

Her sister Mlle Schuppe. Deceased.

Guéguen . . . . Mme Guéguen (Breton woman in her sixties) Deported August 15 1944. Deceased.

H

Hélène . . . . One of my sisters in the réseau "C.N.D. Castille", arrested October 15, 1942, liberated from Romainville February 28, 1944.

Hilde . . . . German prisoner, asocial kapo of the wood column.

Hoffmann . . . . . . Protestant pastor, visited the sick deportees in the Swedish hospitals.

I

Irène. . . . . Mme Tillion (called Irène) arrested in August 1942 (despite her age of 65 years), was my companion in the cell at la Santé for 8 days, passed through Fresnes, Romainville and Compiègne. Deported January 1944. Deceased

Mother of Germaine Tillion, called Koury. Deported. Returned. Repatriated by Sweden.

Isabelle. . . . . My youngest sister in the réseau "C.N.D. Castille," arrested June 13 1942. Deported August 15 1944, was included as was I, in the commando of Rechlin. Returned. Repatriated by Sweden.

J

Jackson. . . . . Mme Jackson (called Toquette). Deported August 15 1944, included in the Commandos of Torgaü and Petit-Kœnigsberg. Returned. Repatriated by Sweden.

Her husband, Doctor Jackson, head doctor of the American hospital at Neuilly. Deported to Neuengamme. Died in the shipwreck at Lübeck.

Her son, Philippe Jackson. Deported to Neuengamme. Returned (survivor of the shipwreck at Lübeck.

Jacqueline . . . . . . One of my sisters in the réseau "C.N.D. Castille." Arrested October 15 1942, freed from Romainvile February 28, 1944.

Jean-Luc. . . . . Son of my brother Gilbert, dead at 14 months.

Jeanne . . . . Called "La grande Jeanne". Deported. Hired on the wood column. Deceased.

Jeannot. . . . . Mme Wackherr (called Jeannot or Good Mama) in the réseau "C.N.D. Castille", arrested June 10, 1942. Deported April 27 1943. Returned. Repatriated by Sweden.

Jeff . . . . See Dixon.

Josiane . . . . Companion in Ravensbrück. Returned.

K

Koury . . . . See Germaine (daughter of Iréne).

See Tillion.

L

Labussière . . . . . . Mme Labussière. Deported to Ravensbrück in May 1944. although sick and old. Deceased.

Her husband was also deported. Returned.

Lachaud. . . . . Mme Lachaud. Deported May 15 1944. One daughter deported. (I don't know if they returned).

Laprade . . . . Mme de Laprade. Deported to Ravensbrück in May 1944, despite her great age. Deceased.

A son was also deported. Deceased.

Laurent . . . . Madeleine Laurent, in the réseau "C.N.D. Castille", arrested June 10 1942. Deported to Ravensbrück April 27 1943. Returned. Repatriated by Switzerland.
Sister of Michèle (see Facq). Deported. Returned.
Daughter of Madame Laurent, in the réseau, "C.N.D. Castille", arrested June 10 1942 (65 years old and blind). Deceased in the cell at Fresnes in 1942 during the week of Christmas.

Lily . . . . Countess of Rambuteau. Deported to Ravensbrück August 15, 1944. Returned. Repatriated by Sweden.
Two sons deported. Returned.
Her husband deported. Deceased.

Lotte . . . . Lotte von Zeissl (Viennese). Deported August 15, 1944. Returned.

Lucienne . . . . See Dixon.

M

Madeleine . . . . . . One of my sisters (called Matelot by our family) in the réseau "C.N.D. Castille", arrested October 15 1942, freed from Romainville February 28, 1944, nearly died from the consequences of her detention.

Maine . . . . Maine Winisdorfer (Mme Berr) arrested in March 1942. Deported to Ravensbrück at the end of January 1944. Returned. Maine was head of the camp of French women at Romainville. This post permitted her to assist several prisoners. She agreed to pass to the men's side, by hiding it in a package of laundry, the telegram that I had received in a parcel, so that my brother Philippe and his friends could have current news. This parcel was brought to the Commander of Romainville by Huguette François, wife of Louis François, of the réseau "C.N.D. Castille".

Maisie . . . . The affectionate name used by my family and friends; my real name is May.

Maman . . . . My mother, in the réseau "C.N.D. Castille" arrested October 15 1942 with my brother Philippe and my sisters Hèléne, Jacqueline and Madeleine—Isabelle and I had been arrested previously; they were freed from Romainville February 28, 1944.

Manuel . . . . Son of my brother Gilbert. Died at 18 months, Christmas night 1942.

Maria . . . . German prisoner, kapo.

Marion. . . . . One of the daughters of Philippe, only three months old at the time of her father's arrest.

Marila. . . . . Czech prisoner, kapo at Rechlin.

Matelot . . . . Diminutive given by our family to my sister Madeleine.

Melot . . . . Mme Melot (Belgian). Deported to Ravensbrück. Deceased. Her husband M. Melot, deported. Deceased. Three daughters deported: Madeleine, returned; Claire returned; Suzanne deceased.

Michèle . . . . Oldest daughter of my brother Phillipe, she was three at the time of her father's arrest.

Mickie . . . . Mme Poirier (called Mickie). Deported to Ravensbrück (employee of the work bureau). Returned. Repatriated by Sweden.

Monet . . . . Mme Monet, Deported to Ravensbrück in May 1944, although sick and old. Deceased.

N

Nicole. . . . . Nicole de Witasse. Deported August 15 1944. Attempted to escape at Lagny with Alix d'Unienville when the tracks cut by the Maquis forced us to travel on foot across the countryside to another station. Alix d'Unienville succeeded, Nicole was recaptured, included in the commandos of Torgaü and Petit-Kœnigsbeg, returned to Ravensbrück at the evacuation of Petit-Kœnigsberg. Deceased.

O

Odette . . . . Companion of Rechlin, killed during the heavy bombing of the airfield.

P

Philippe . . . . My brother in the reséau "C.N.D. Castille"; father of Michèle and Marion, arrested October 15 1942. Deported in May 1944. Died in the shipwreck at Lübeck, May 3 1945.

Pierre . . . . Paul Mauger, called Mimi, called Pierre, called Rodolphe in the réseau "C.N.D. Castille," personal agent of my brother Colonel Rémy, arrested May 30 1942. Deported March 1943 to Mathausen, Returned.

Pierrette. . . . . Pierrette Henriot. Deported to Ravensbrück at the beginning of 1944, included in the commando of Rechlin. Deceased.

R

Rambuteau . . . . . See Lily.

Raspilaire. . . . . . . Mme Raspilaire. Deported to Ravensbrück in May 1944, although very old. Deceased.

Rousseau . . . . Jean Rousseau, friend of my brother Philippe. Deported to Neuengamme, hospitalized at Lund, Sweden, was one of the first to speak of the drama at Lübeck. Returned.

S

Schuppe. . . . . Mlle Schuppe, sister of Mme Grüner. Deported August 15 1944, included in the commandos of Torgaü and Petit-Kœnigsberg, returned to Ravensbrück at the evacuation of this last commando. Deceased, as was her sister Mme Grüner.

Sparre. . . . . Countess Sparre, daughter of the former French minister to Sweden, M. Bernard, devotedly visited the Swedish hospitals and quarantine camps at the time of liberating the concentration camps; gave news of the repatriation of my brother Philippe, according to the information available at that time.

Numerous Swedes were equally devoted; Prince Wilhelm of Sweden himself made efforts to find the disappeared.

Others include Mmes. Norlander, Britt Aschan, Ostberg (wife of a doctor at the hospital of Växjö), Mme Fricq, Mlle Webel, Baron Carl de Geer and many whose names I don't know.

Superior. . . . . Mother Superior of the Compassion of Lyon. Deported early 1944. Deceased.

Suzanne. . . . . Suzanne, daughter of Mme Melot. Deported. Deceased.

T

Talet........... Mlle Talet, directress of the high school at Angers. Deported end of January 1944. Deceased.

Tillion .... See Irène.

Toquette........ See Jackson.

V

Vachon.......... Mlle Vachon. Deported August 15 1944. Deceased.

Von Zeissl ...... See Lotte.

W

Witasse .... See Nicole.

Names of Germans

Binz .... [Dorothea Binz] Head guard, female, having high functions in the camp; showed the greatest ferocity toward the prisoners; arrested at the liberation; condemned to death at the Ravensbrück trial. Hung.

Kratz .... German sub officer, he functioned as cook at the Fort of Romainville, but in reality he belonged to the SD (Sicherheitsdienst), a German security and intelligence agency of the SS.

Pflaum.......... [Hans Pflaum] German officer nicknamed "merchant of cows." At Ravensbrück, he designated the women able to go on work transports; together with the doctor he made the selections for the gas chamber; had a reputation for his cruelty and was arrested at the liberation; interned at Neuengamme; escaped. [He was recaptured in 1949 and sentenced to death in the 1950 French military trial at Rastatt.]

Names of Hostages Held at Ravensbrück

during repatriation and claimed individually
by Count Bernadotte.

Countess Jacqueline d'Alincourt.
Countess Jeanne de Bertier
Mlle Christiane de Cuverville.
Baroness de Dumas.
Countess de Gontaut-Biron.
Mlle Béatrix de Gontaut-Biron.
Gereral Lelong.
Mlle Jacqueline Lelong.
Madame Massensier.
Madame Annie Renaud de Saint-Georges.
Mlle Isabelle Renault.
Mlle Maisie Renault.
Madame Tritz.
And two Polish women whose names are unknown.

Appendix

Meaning of foreign words, specifically German words, in the narrative.

Achtung . . . . Attention.
Arbeitseinstaz . . . . Translated in the narrative as "work bureau."
Aufseherin . . . . Guard, in this case a female guard.
Aufseherinnen . . . . Plural of *Aufseherin*.
Blockälteste . . . . Proper meaning: head of the block; at Rechlin improperly designating a woman prisoner who functions as head of the camp.
Blockowa . . . . Head of the block (office filled by a prisoner).
Fliegeralarm . . . . Translated in the narrative as "alert" (air raid warning).
Holzkolonne . . . . Translated in the narrative as "wood column."
Kammer/Kammern . . . . . Translated in the narrative as "store/stores."
Kapo . . . . Prisoner who is in charge of a work detail.
Lagerstrasse . . . . Main street of the camp.
Morgen . . . . Translated in the narrative as "morning."
Revier. . . . . Translated in the narrative as "Infirmary."
Schmutzstück . . . . Explained in the narrative as "dirty bits," a term used to describe the wretched, hopeless persons who had abandoned all "decorum."
Sönderführer . . . . German officer involved with police and intelligence matters.
Stubowa . . . . Head of the room (filled by a prisoner).
Strafblock . . . . Translated in the narrative as "punishment block."
Waschraum . . . . Washroom.
Wehrmacht . . . . German Armed Forces.
Voralarm . . . . Translated in the narrative as "pre-alert."
Zulage . . . . Translated in the narrative as "supplement."
Jugendlager. . . . . Youth camp; at Ravensbrück, originally a camp for young Germans; later where the old women and sick were sent for extermination.
N/N (Nacht und Nebel). . . Night and Fog. [This Decree of 1941 had the intent of causing political activists to disappear, so no information could be found on their whereabouts or fate.]

[Translator's additions:]

Bekleidung . . . . Clothing
Kreigsmarine. . . . . German Navy 1935–1945
Luftwaffe . . . . German Air Force 1935–1945

UNIVERSITY OF
Nebraska
Lincoln

www.ingramcontent.com/pod-product-compliance
Lightning Source LLC
LaVergne TN
LVHW091000080826
845145LV00003B/1068